FaL's Boy

A Treatise

Of Conjecture On The True Nature Of God

outskirts
press

A Treatise of Conjecture on the True Nature of God
All Rights Reserved.
Copyright © 2020 FaL's Boy
v4.0

The opinions expressed in this manuscript are solely the opinions of the author and do not represent the opinions or thoughts of the publisher. The author has represented and warranted full ownership and/or legal right to publish all the materials in this book.

This book may not be reproduced, transmitted, or stored in whole or in part by any means, including graphic, electronic, or mechanical without the express written consent of the publisher except in the case of brief quotations embodied in critical articles and reviews.

Outskirts Press, Inc.
http://www.outskirtspress.com

Paperback ISBN: 978-1-9772-2837-6
Hardback ISBN: 978-1-9772-3433-9

Cover Photo © 2020 www.gettyimages.com. All rights reserved - used with permission.

Outskirts Press and the "OP" logo are trademarks belonging to Outskirts Press, Inc.

PRINTED IN THE UNITED STATES OF AMERICA

Table of Contents

TO BE GOD OR NOT TO BE GOD 1
THE HYPE OF WISDOM REVEALED………. 11
AND THEN THERE'S JOB…………….................................17
FEAR…….. WHY FEAR? 21
NOW, LET"S TAKE A LOOK AT KING SOLOMON………. ...29
WEALTH………………………………………………………….33
ATTENTION……………………………………………………...39
SEX………...41
DRUGS……………………………………………………………53
GETTING OUT OF THE WEEDS……….............................63

Foreword

RARE, INDEED, IS wisdom so finely distilled from an elder sage than that which is found in this treatise. This work knits the wisdom of the ages with current events to produces a keen and precise discernment of the times in which we live. This treatise places the traditional paradigmic myths of black inferiority and white privilege under the Light of Biblical history, in search of an answer to Marvin Gaye's question, "What's going on?"

There is a haunting depth of understanding on the question of the nature of God as He relates to man. You will experience a poetic message, the crux of which is that the Creator was intentional not only in making Black people, but has a much larger plan in play, which He states as culmination in an Eternal Kingdom. When God decided to make Israelites into His Chosen People, the Creator summoned the heads of the 12 tribes of Israel to Africa, (by Joseph), along with their 56 male offspring, totaling 68 Hebrew males and the only 2 Hebrew females; Israel's raped daughter Dinah and his granddaughter named Serah. Only these 70 souls comprised God's Chosen people who were prophesied by God to spend 400 years enslaved in "the land of Ham" aka Egypt. (Ps. 105:23)

These Chosen People, after becoming a large body of people, and enslaved out of fear by the Pharaoh, were then called out of Africa by God using Moses, who could easily , based on his African ancestry, assume the position of an African in the high court of Pharaoh, though he was in actuality a Hebrew, adopted by the daughter of Pharaoh. And like Moses, the millions of enslaved Hebrews had the colored appearance as their African masters in "the land of Ham" because the 56 Hebrew bachelors mated with Egypt's Hamites over that 400 years of servitude. Therefore, the people that Moses brought out of African slavery were a colored people, called *a mixed multitude*. (Ex. 12:38, 2:5-11; Ps 106:22)

In the Old Testament, the Creator's constant boast to Israel is how He had delivered them as His Chosen People "out of the land of Egypt, out of the house of bondage" from the world's first superpower. Hebrews, being a stiffed-necked people, began serving idol gods of Ham's cursed Canaanites, which moved God to jealousy. (Gen. 9:18) God promised to "scatter" his Chosen People throughout the world in such a way that wherever they were found they would be discriminated against and persecuted. One tribe of Israelites, after leaving Africa, intermarried with the tribe of Noah's great grandson by Japheth, the father of the Caucasians, named "Ashkenaz". (Gen. 10:2-3) These Hebrews call themselves Ashkenazi Jews. They are the white Jews of Europe, and the world still talks of the mistreatment they endured in Hitler's slave camps, as prophesied by Moses in the curses laid out in Deuteronomy 28 for Hebrews who defected from the faith of the God of Israel. But, they are only part of *one* tribe, the tribe of Judah, who became "light skinned" by intermarrying with Europeans of Germany many years after Jesus Christ, the Lion of Judah, was born. Where are the other ten "lost tribes of Hebrews" that were scattered? This work brings to the forefront the clues that the curse in Deuteronomy provides, and using it as a template, one can easily see that the other ten tribes may very well be represented as that same "mixed multitude", African Hebrews, the Erverh, (Eber), descendants of their father, Shem, (Genesis 10:21).

When reading the curses of the particular type of slavery that God promised would overtake Hebrews that apostatized, meaning defected from His Covenants, one can discover, by beginning from that Old Testament point of Deuteronomy 28 and moving forward to Christ in the New Testament, the beginning of a black history of black people who were sold from Africa by Africans, not as their brothers, but as non-assimilating Hebrews to endure the curse of slavery until they returned back to the God of Israel. As the Temple was central to Hebrews of Old, the Church is central to colonial free Hebrews today. This is a work whose time has come.

James H. Warden, Jr. Th.M.
Author of The Complete Works of Blacks in the Bible

Acknowledgements

THANK YOU, MOM, and Dad. For simply giving me the opportunity to be myself long enough to find out who I am. Parenting? I never knew you were doing that. I thought you were just being who you were! What a way to discover that you are loved.

Thank you, Joe, Monique, and Melanie, for giving me the opportunity to pay that love forward, and to you Emma, for being the glue that bound us all together.

Everyone plays a part in the life of each we know. We come to understand each other, as we come to realize that love is first taught by being loved, and is culminated in, fulfilled in, loving one another. To list each by name is necessary, for all have played a part in my life experience, but to do so would require an order of importance, a lengthy explanation of the significance each has had on my self understanding, a task I am truly not capable of doing. You each know, and I attest to the fact that during many times in my life I have reflected on each of your interactions with me, some of those were trying experiences, some elating, some educational, and they all, each and every experience, have come together as good, and worthy. Know that you were and are a part of the village that brought me love, and I thank you all for that love.

To my family, all, I know you, and you know me. I am so glad to be a part of the legacy that we are. Carters, our Carters, are a conglomeration of many, but we have come together to become a family, inspired by those 10, ….JT, Floyd, Nicee, Florence, BK, Cat, Fred, Sis, Tom, and Cal.

Life is experience, and each experience is a dot. Connecting the dots will reveal a clue to the essence of what life is, and family can be one of the richest sources of dots one can have when learning what living is about. I thank God for the measure of understanding our family has received, and I thank my family for valuing that gift, and keeping it in our experience with each other.

And last, and most importantly, I thank God for the path of understanding, carved through the ages, and culminated in the message of Christ, helping us all to come to know the Truth that sets us free to live eternally.

Foreword to Treatise

A LIFETIME. SEEMS like a lifetime is an era. And I suppose that every person experiences the time of the life they live as though it is an era. History is being made in the minds of many, and that history is exactly what that word, as assembled letters, would mean. His story. His story is Her story as well. Nothing unique about that assessment. The story of mankind is complex, varied, literally too big to detail. It has been summed up in many ways. The Weltanschauung, world view, a man develops, and accepts, is unavoidable, but nevertheless confounding. To quote a man discussed in this treatise, "there is nothing new under the sun." Yet we all look at the same picture, and we each see things with eyes that detail a slightly different image. That image we see is different, because it is that part of the picture that includes our selves.

I have to ask myself, when I take those words to heart, then why does anything matter? If there is nothing new, then what is there? That, the search for what is and what matters, is what I have come to realize we each are required to define for ourselves. Newness, is a relative term in our modern understanding. We have allowed the concept of New to be morphed into a panacea. We boldly search for new answers to problems, find new "paradigms" of understanding, push the limits of science, technology, believing that by doing so, we will find a breakthrough into a better world,…. It is a very subtle distortion of faith.

To look beyond that which is, in search of something better, seems a useful endeavor. There is even proof that the search for "better" has brought many "improvements" in the lives of mankind. Antibiotic therapy, electricity, oil and the internal combustion engine, space exploration and satellite technology, nuclear medicine, nano technology, genetic modification, …….there is a very long list of things that have brought a "better" life to mankind.

Yet, no matter how innovative these discoveries are, or how useful, valuable they have become, the point made is that there is nothing new, and that point is most likely not referring to a simple look around and noticing that everything "known" is known, and things not yet discovered will not change the way things are. At any given time, the lives of man can change because of a discovery, a new way of looking at a given system, or principle. Change, is change. Different is different. New, is not even conceptual. Something that was not, and now is. That is new. There is not even a word for whatever is new. You have to be able to speak about that which did not exist, but has become real, and therefore is, in order to say that it is new. Most of the time, new is just something that is different, but the same. A new car model. It is new, but a car is not something new. A new suit. It is new, just finished, and hung on the sale rack, but it might look a lot like a lot of other suits, because suits are a well known item. Classified as apparel. Different variations already. Double breasted, pleated pants or skirt, men's or women's, tuxedo, summer, all kinds already.

So King Solomon may have been making a statement about something else when he said that there is nothing "new" under the sun. Under the sun seems to be a phrase that expresses a broad understanding. In that first chapter of Ecclesiastes, Solomon, the writer, is basically letting the reader know that he is reflecting on the nature of all things. The labors a man has performed over his lifetime; generations which are born, live, and die, and soon are forgotten; the sun perpetually rising and falling; the wind forever blowing here and there; rivers flowing forever into the sea but the sea never filling. He poses these things, I believe, to say that he is commenting on the very nature of the world, as he sees it. There is nothing new under the sun. Can this be said in another way?

Our ability to affect the world around us does not mean that we have any understanding of a positive or negative effect on the world. Because we are able to change things does not mean we are able to make meaningful changes. Specifically, we can point to many instances of positive change, negative change, as well as "no change", all occurring in the same world, at the same time. We can point to innovations in transportation, and the effect of moving from horse drawn buckboards and wagons to powered crafts that allow us access to every corner of the earth as well as Space, yet we cannot find justice for everyone, food for the hungry, opportunity for those who only need an opportunity. For every advancement, there seems to remain a never ending setback. Farmers produce enough food to feed the world, yet millions of people die each year from starvation, and billions of pounds of food are literally disposed of without feeding anyone. The richest countries in the world have many, many people living in poverty. We increase the lifespan of people through medical "miracles" and better living conditions, yet the quality of life even for the rich can oftentimes be worse than the daily life of those who struggle daily to meet the daily requirements of living. To King Solomon, as well as to us, the solutions to our problems have not brought some of the most desired changes, and even if the desired changes do occur, the sum total of our experience with living is often not impacted in any lasting way. Even that which we can describe as wonderful to experience is limited in scope, and all seems to be fixed in ways contrary to what seems to be the desired experience. Those who seem to be contented with life have no reproducible formula to provide for others to achieve the contentment they exude. There are no limits to exceptions to a given rule. There are no rules which apply to all instances. Nuance is the fly in the ointment of the "law of the land". The same act can produce a different result, and the desired result may never seem to occur, even with repeated effort.

And so it goes. With every summary judgement of one's "world view", the world seems relentless in declaring that view not relative to more and more instances viewed within the context of the very "world view" lens one judged as correct, and relatively comprehensive. So. And so it goes, except when it doesn't go that way. And that's the way it is, sometimes. Other times, it is a different way. That's the way it is today, pretty much.

It is very hard to express this concept, but let me use Solomon to help, for just a few items. One man had 700 wives and 300 concubines. A thousand women to fulfill his heart's desire. Would 17 more wives, and maybe, 41 more concubines have done the trick for him? The story, his story, is that the queen of Sheba, Makeda, was the love of his life. Not only Biblical, but the story has historical roots in the history of Ethiopia, which to this day claims a direct lineage to this King. Today, nothing much is known about Solomon's first wife, except her name, Naamah, and the fact that she was a Pharoah's daughter. Even less is known about Solomon's 37th wife, let alone his 699th wife. The Biblical account of Solomon's life gives the most detail and seeming importance to his relationship with Makeda, and not as much to the other 1000 women in his life. Based on the constraints of respect for the law during those times, is it possible that the Song of Solomon is not going to spell out with names and minute detail the relationship the King of Israel had with a woman from another country who would be damaged by having his child, but would rather identify her as a Shulamite woman, and himself as the king.

Nevertheless, the Song of Solomon exists in the Holy Bible, if no one else other than God thought it "appropriate". Nothing is new under the sun, the phrase that expressed the vision of the life of King Solomon. Was he trying to say that everything is simply what it is,....or maybe, nothing is ever what it seems, ... nothing retains its' significance,.....there is a seemingly infinite number of variations on a theme, but the melody remains……. There is a lot under the sun, but the more it changes, the more it remains the same. He was expressing utter confoundment with his perspective on life itself.

I say that to say that when we record, recollect a story of someone, that story is told from the teller's perspective. When we state a memorable name, Columbus, Abraham Lincoln, George Wallace, Martin Luther King, Socrates, King George, Albert Einstein, John Wayne, Marilyn Monroe, Harriet Tubman, Eunice Carter, George Patton, Mr. Rogers, …….. even fictitious names like James Bond, John Shaft, Batman, Matt Dillon, Perry Mason, all these names conjure up specific understandings about them. In the case of those real individuals, certain thoughts come to mind, and in some cases the facts as well as the truth of those "facts" are in dispute, or proven false. Nevertheless, both the truth and the truth dispelled can be known. Thus the import from our understanding, notwithstanding the fact and fiction, both about real and fictitious people, is what we retain as belief about them, and sometimes remaining in error, our understanding of these people remains flawed. Even our notion of the legal system becomes influenced by the antics of Perry Mason in the fictitious courtroom, winning every case. Knowing that it is all illusion and fictitious, it still feels in a way real to us, and lodges into our consciousness as well as our unconscious understanding of the workings of the law. Abraham Lincoln freed the slaves, though he didn't. Columbus discovered America, though it had been inhabited for thousands of years, all women found James "Sean Connery" Bond irresistible, (maybe not?). And then there is Eunice Carter, who doesn't even exist in the minds of very many people at all, a Black woman, lawyer, daughter of slaves, who took down Mafia boss Lucky Luciano. I threw in that tidbit about Eunice Carter not because there is any connection between us, I only know of her because of curiosity in a book written about her by her relative. She will become to me whatever I read about her in the book. And those words, written by her relative, will most likely be the only basis of my belief in her existence. Not ever having met her, and not knowing whether she is, was real, somehow, she will be, in a way, created by her relative. Much the same way Ronald Reagan created the "welfare queen", Linda Taylor, a real woman in Chicago, who was the person he conjured into an alternate existence, for political purposes. It was an easy exaggeration to make, because it fit into a racial narrative about Black Americans that had been going on for hundreds of years.

Do we know Linda Taylor better by accepting her as the "welfare queen", or by reading the story of her life by a somewhat impartial journalist. Do we understand America better by believing that he, Columbus, "discovered" a Continent and called it America, or by the history of the indigenous people who inhabited the continent for many thousands of years? Do we understand mankind better by what is written by him, or by what is written about him? Who can write about man but man himself? What a ridiculous notion? Well, on cave and tomb paintings, writings on stone, pottery, possibly as long as we have come to realize that we have a consciousness, there has been a message shared with man by Someone who knows him, and knows him well. He has come to be known as God, and has survived many derivatives of man's speculation as well as documentation of

Him, and His will. As I said earlier, books relate facts from the writer's perspective. We error in thinking that the Bible is a book written by man. To anyone who doubts it, there is much stated in the Bible by those who penned it, literal quotes from many storied in the Bible, that point out God's direct words, in detail, both involving the nature of man, specific commands and prophecies, errors in man's thinking, and His, God's purpose in all that has occurred, is occurring, and will occur in the "end times'" It is about time we look at those words, for they have purpose, and source.

A TREATISE OF CONJECTURE ABOUT THE TRUE NAURE OF GOD

by Fals' Boy

I AM HAUNTED by the notion that the God of the Bible is not color blind. God, who is not to be mocked, knew Hebrew Israel. God knew each and every one of them, because those are the people with whom He shared His message. His message? I am. Before this was written in Scripture, it was shared, as a divine statement of His reality, to His Creation, Adam, and Eve. There was a world of men, and women, who knew that there was a God, and worshipped Him. They sacrificed on altars to Him. They "called on the name of the Lord", before there was a word written in the Bible. Were Adam and Eve the very first of His creation? I suspect not because of one word. Replenish. (Genesis 1:28). Though translated in many different ways, most likely misunderstood in as many, that word stands, translated correctly in many translations I suspect, suggesting that there was something, someone, before. Whether by an erroneous translation, or by divine intervention, without that word, one still must understand that there is a history referred to but not detailed in the Genesis account. Archaeology, science, and even Scripture agree. As a matter of fact, there is much that predates the beginning of the history recorded in the Bible. There is much that provides evidence of the notion of God, relating to man, prior to the writing of Genesis. That history does not deny God, but does not identify Him as He is identified in Holy Scripture. But whatever was, before the creation of Adam and Eve, that history, some of which we have uncovered, vanished into what was simply described as a part of the "earth being without form, and darkness was on the face of the deep." Dinosaurs were, but they haven't been for a long time, and longing for them, and whatever and who or whomever was here with them, is not very relevant to, but certainly is a part of the creation of this "system of things" we refer to as the Solar System. The Creator who could write the entire book of the "System", has pointed us to the portion of this "System" that concerns us, and the Bible is that guide.

I find it rather odd that there is very little speculation on the origin of many written artifacts that resemble phrases from the Bible. There are historians, archaeologists, minds that seek truth,...Diop ben jochannan, Rogers, Imhotep, Sertima, Windsor, Israel, Cummings, Jackson, Clarke, Warden, Budge, many others, who have unearthed much evidence of reference to a god in African societies that predates the Biblical flood, and even predates the assumed time of the beginning with Adam. This evidence is resisted because it is thought to challenge the Bible's veracity. I find that one word to be meaningful, replenish, because it helps place the Bible in a historical context that allows a continuum of the quest God has to develop a people to inhabit His Kingdom. If we can acknowledge efforts by God in the Old Testament to establish a relationship with the Nation of Israel, which, according to Scripture, was fraught with denial, falling away, disbelief, even in the midst of miraculous events, (parting seas, plaques on Pharaoh, manna, etc. etc.), why would it be impossible to entertain the possibility of God's interaction with His prior creative acts leaving evidence of the impact God had on the lives of people in a world who knew nothing of a concept of god? I can easily imagine people, completely new to the concept of there being a "god", deciding that because there is one, there are probably others. People deciding that a miracle experienced might be explainable in other ways, believing that other gods may be the cause of things happening. I can imagine people inventing ideas about what actions will produce the power of a god, worshipping something or someone else in hopes of getting help in a fashion similar to the way God responded to those, the Israelites, with whom He sought a relationship. The continuum of God's interaction with man detailed in the Bible may be just the tail end of a much longer struggle God has had with man, who was created and didn't have any formalized concept of God. I believe the beginning is truly the beginning. God created the heavens and the earth.

The word "now", (Genesis 1:2), also seems purposeful. I think we all too easily consider that word as just the beginning of a sentence. But it is not possible to create something, and then refer to it already being in a certain condition. Somehow, I think that the word "now" in Genesis 1:2, is placed to move us forward. How far forward? To the creation of New people, Adam and Eve? From the wheel to the wagon to the car to the bullet train. If we want to explore the modern bullet train, we may very well refer to early evidence of man's desire to move himself, or things. But we would use a phrase such as "now", to suggest that let's get right into the development of the bullet train, and not spend thousands of pages covering the wheel, engine etc,.... Can we, as creatures living today, truly think that we can understand the beginning of things? All things? Everything that has occurred since time began? We have come to understand the building blocks of life itself, DNA, RNA, and how to finagle clones by zapping living components with electrical charges, not creating but kick starting the machinery that has been running on autopilot since the inception of mankind. Does cloning mean we know how to create? Or does it mean that we know how to finagle? How far removed can our understanding be from a Creator who develops that which is not, into something that is us, versus our absence of the concept, design, and manufacturing of a cosmos within which we are a minute part? Everything living, according to the Genesis account, is simply spoken into existence. Man is the only part of the creation that is formed from the ground, and has life "breathed" into him. Thus life, the ability to become a living thing, is a pronouncement into reality for everything except Adam, and then, Eve. The building blocks work for everything living. The "leggos" used are the same pieces for plants, cows, and mankind, but they are compiled in different ways to create a living world. All that grows, reproduces, and dies is perpetual in that process. It, that process, never ends with the "death" of individual blades of grass, goats, or mankind, unless there is a complete destruction of all that is defined by the expression of the DNA structure. Extinction is the only way to stop the continuum of living.

What this thought leads me to, however, is the validity in paying attention to words placed in the historical narrative. The Book of the Dead, some of the very early writings, the stone carvings, ….are these things evidence of people grappling with the concepts presented to an earlier man by God? We know that there were people who did not believe in the concept of god, and we know that the Nation of Israel had been exposed to idol "gods" from the Egyptians. And where did they, the Egyptians, get that concept? The Pharaoh does not question the concept of a god when Moses states he wants to go away and worship his God. He is comfortable with the concept. Did the Egyptians just make it up, the idea of god, or see it displayed and attempt to copy it? Mankind's first experience with God may not necessarily have been the experience in Genesis. The Radio Shack model one computer, with 4 k memory and a cassette tape recorder for storage, was a computer. There have been many advances in the computer since the "Univac". We allow ourselves to experience development. We do not, however, accept God developing a relationship with man, and that relationship beginning before the creation of Adam and Eve. We proudly display the 1st computer in a museum, and pride ourselves on how far we have come. The landfills and waste dumps have become, in a real sense, a version of what we might understand as our version of the phrase "without form…. darkness on the face of the deep..". We create, yet do not allow ourselves to consider the possibility that our Creator had been creating before we became! There are Scriptures in Job that suggest this very concept as fact. So. Let's pay attention to the words in Scripture, and see if they can not only lead us to God, but to our history with Him.

In paying attention to the history of the Israelite Nation, we must not fail to make a reasonable assumption. God kept track of His people, the Hebrew Israelites, whom He delivered out of bondage and into the Promised Land. He spoke to them through the prophets, through Moses, Joshua, others. He had a very powerful ongoing relationship with His people, and they were given guidance, protection, and were watched over. He has, through prophets, outlined what is to be everlasting as a Kingdom. Not in every day detail. The narrowness of the human mind ought be willing to accept the vastness of a Creator, and be willing to allow for the possibility of our specific experienced human existence to literally be represented by a "nanosecond" in time, like a snapshot of a cell mutation. A comprehensive "recollection" of each of our lifetimes, pieced together in a book, condensed to important scenes that represent experiences we each consider worthy of mention, would be like dots representing our existence; those dots, when connected only represent connected dots, not who we are, let alone how we fit into the bigger picture of the picture that is all that is, ….. and then, seen in entirety, by a Creator. The BOOK OF THE COSMOS, in every detail, placing all in its proper place, and sequence, cannot be written, and even more importantly, cannot be SUMMARIZED! If we, as humans, make one mistake that I fear clouds much of our understanding, it is the tendency to fall prey to the generalization of knowledge from algorithmic leaning supposition. We think we see what we see, and then we check to see if that is what we see. That is impossible. We don't know what we don't know, so we seek to determine if what we see can become something we can know. At some level, the biochemical reactions that occur within us become thoughts that in turn create more reactions that grow into a complex thing we call, for lack of a better word, understanding. That understanding may lead to a Conclusion. And every conclusion has the potential to become a future road block, and every such road block can become the guide to a new understanding. And every understanding, can lead to a conclusion,………. Yes. It can go round and round, and that is because we have a limited concept of what is. And why do we have that? We desperately need it, because otherwise, we have no foundation within which we can survive daily as people. We need a mutuality to survive with each other. Yet, what have we done, with all that has come before us as information, knowledge, history, progress……. We have turned life, into "LIFE", the game! Monopoly, the game. Our "world view" has become an incessant babbling about jobs, education, environment, marriage, family, health, the economy, housing, infrastructure, politics, foreign relations, religion, mores, traditions, culture, manufacturing, service, war, recession, depression, addiction, sexuality, morality, …… isn't this list itself rather depressing? A new layer of fat collects in the arteries with each word. A grey hair, or a lost hair, is somehow connected to each one of the "terms" that I failed to list. Like what? Like,… love, friendship, concern, faithfulness, loyalty, happiness, contentment, ……… and each one of these words brings the reality of a hair gone gray, or south, swept away with the lack of attention paid to things that really matter. And what does this whole line of thinking have to do with God? Everything. Not just the concept of God, but a reality of God that places meaning over a lived life.

So we find, in the Bible, more than in any other Book of its kind, a following of man, as man follows God. An enlightenment of man, as man comes to understand that God has a road map for living. A God that claims a people as one He will reign over, and through that people He will accomplish something He desires,.......a blessed World. It is in that detail, I find identity with those who struggled with the concept of God being God. The Israelites. And the detail He, God, chose not to allow us to miss, is that disobeying Him, and failing to live by His word, is a serious assault to His purposes. That is the message in Deuteronomy. If you accept Me, I will be your God. You don't even know what a God is. But accept what I say, and things will go as I planned, and you will thrive and be forever glad you did. If you do not, you, and your offspring, for what is truly an eternity to you, will live in misery. Not because I will make your life miserable as a punishment, but because without Me your life is meaningless, miserable, of no value.

The Israelites know what God told them, and they knew who He meant those words to touch. God also knows who are the offspring of the Nation of Israel, because He, being all knowing, continued to watch them over the years, having had to leave them to their own devices, because of their unbelief in Him. Warning them what would happen to them, and explaining to them what would be the future of the world they inhabited if they disobeyed Him and turned away from Him, God sent His son, Jesus, after these "lost" souls, in what has to be the "Last days". He knows the offspring of the Hebrew Israelites better than they know themselves. To think otherwise, would be to mock God. Surely we can't think that He would "lose track" of the remnant of the Hebrew nation that has been scattered to the ends of the earth by God himself? Not scattered by His power, but by their wandering, away from His protection and into a world inhabited by the "Prince of the power of the air".

Therefore, I resolve to follow this course to its inevitable conclusion. In these end times, which have Jesus allowing a recording of His prayer with His Father, (Gospel of John), we find Jesus stating He has those whom God, His Father, has instructed him to find, and He gives them to the Hands of the Father. These men, the disciples and the others who are part of the Church of believers, are to go into the world and teach all nations, baptizing, bringing this new hope to the Lost of Israel, who in turn bring the Gospel to the Gentiles.

To think that God does not know whom He seeks, is an affront. It matters not what is considered truth, for God is the author of TRUTH, and He, through parables, Prophets, and His Son, has come, at this time, to claim those who were His people, and bring them back together, and to Him, and His Kingdom. He intends for all who believe in Him to be saved and given everlasting life, just as all who were part of the Hebrew nation, whether by purchase, or as servants, or strangers who became a part of the household, all who were under the roof of an Israelite, became part of the Nation of Israel. Males were circumcised, because they were under the Nation of Israel. Those males, and their family members, were a part of the Nation. Likewise, all who accept Jesus as savior are part of the Kingdom. So it would be foolish to think that God, after declaring to those Patriarchs to make all people affiliated with them a part of the Hebrew Nation, will seek only those who are genetically affiliated to be considered part of the Lost.

By that same token, there are a lot of Hamites who became part of the Hebrew Nation through marriage and purchase, and they, therefore, are part of those who are lost. We cannot claim to accept any discretion regarding the Lost of Israel. God did not make any distinction between those who were part of the nation by birth, and those who were part of the nation by affiliation. Thousands of years later, which to God, may only represent a few days, surely God in His all knowingness, knows who are the offspring of this nation, and therefore, those whom He warned would suffer the curses in Deuteronomy for their unbelief, through the generations? Why don't we know who they are?

It is not important, I agree in principle, that there be a distinction between the Lost of Israel and those who believe in His son and therefore receive eternal life as a gentile. But I also know, in real terms, that there are actually people, descendants of the Hebrew Israelites, who have been and are suffering the curses of Deuteronomy because of the apostasy of their ancestors, and their unbelief subsequent to that apostasy. And those people, the generations lost because of the unbelief they inherited from their ancestors, may be helped by being given an understanding that they have that rightful place of being those sought after by God, and He will be glad to receive them into His Kingdom. Yes, they must understand that Christ is their savior, but they also must understand that they were to be a blessing to the rest of the world. Ignoring this, is tantamount to once again denying God! You cannot simply think of yourself as a gentile saved by the Gospel! You are a Hebrew Israelite, rescued by the Son, to become a part of the Kingdom, regaining a position you lost through your ancestors' disobedience, and your ignorance to that disobedience. There is no higher status to that claim, but it cannot be ignored!

A man searches for a boat that was lost because his son was on that boat. When he finds it, he rescues all that are on the boat. The life of everyone is saved, and the man is genuinely happy he had found the boat and his efforts have saved all that were aboard. But the son will not act like he is a stranger to his father!!! He will hug his dad, and his dad will hug him, and they will rejoice in each other. All others will rejoice in being found. The relationship between all who were rescued will be anchored in that fact. They will all be thankful to the father for saving them as well as his son, and the father will be overwhelmed with the goodness he has provided by saving the others. They can and will all celebrate this experience. That does not change the fact that the father has a relationship with his son! He was not looking primarily for those who were lost! He was looking for the boat that carried his son,…. That son, whom HE LOST. That is who He defined as LOST! Surely his son appreciated the fact that his father went to great lengths to rescue him, without merely thinking of himself as more valuable than the others in the boat?

So Hebrew Israelites ought be aware of being rescued from the Curse of Deuteronomy, as well as being saved and given eternal life, rescued by the same Savior that instructed those He rescued to go to all nations, teaching, retrieving the Lost and saving the gentile! But are they? Are they aware of who they are? I have to say that since there can be no dispute that the Hebrew Israelite Nation was overwhelmingly made up of Shemites, and possibly the very large majority of that Nation were Hamites, because of century upon century of intermarriage with Hamites, the ancestors of this Nation has to be not only of color, but of what we modernly call the color Black. They were Black people, overwhelmingly. To argue that is to ignore history in favor of deception. Rather than try to prove to a doubting mind that this is true, I would rather suggest to that doubting mind, offer another, MORE reasonable alternative "fact", and preferably one that God Himself might be more willing to accept as fact.

What this revelation might come to mean for African Americans, Haitians, Ghanaians, literally many people of color who may be sought after by the God of Isaac and Jacob, is the only reason for this information to come to light. No one who is Black can bring any good upon themselves by declaring they are part of the "Lost Tribes of Israel". Likewise, no one, by denying the legitimacy of this revelation can usurp the work of reclaiming that has already been done by the Son. The modern research being done by young African Americans and others, rightly bringing to light the facts about the "Lost of Israel" is proof that God is at work responding to the will and work of His son. Therefore, for a Black man to ignore the writings of Scripture, especially without investigating them, is tantamount in many ways to attempting to drive a car blindfolded. Being familiar with a car doesn't mean you can navigate it through traffic blindfolded, ...traffic you cannot see. Many of us are familiar with the Bible as a Book. We have seen it, know it is usually Black, packed with obituaries, dusty, and hard to read. To think of it as being a history of God's relationship with us, people of color, is almost prohibited. Even atheists would balk at that idea. Why that is so is easy to understand? Because,.... God's chosen people have to be white. Period. There would be many more atheists if God's chosen people were people of color. For those who say it doesn't matter what color, (race), they were, I would have to say that if it doesn't matter, then there should be absolutely no resistance to an inquiry into the nature of the Hebrew Israelite community. Historical references, both Biblical and pertinent extra Biblical, ought be used to support the veracity of any inquiry into the nature of the quintessential Hebrew Israelite. My suspicion, if confirmed with the coming of Christ, is that white Christians will have to spend an eternity with people of color, and some will resemble those very people they feared, hated, or vilified. Actually, I would be in error if that were the case. Eternity is not the heavenly time frame nor the realm that Jesus promised to those who didn't love their neighbor as themselves. Likewise, I suspect that realm is not the place where Blacks who desire that whites be punished will see the avenging of those who had condoned and maintained racist views and acts. If ever there was a reason to understand what race bigotry is about, understanding the Biblical import of Deuteronomy is much more relevant than placing blame on whites. Indeed, there may be more value in seeing the world in terms of Deuteronomy if you are the "victim" of race prejudice than seeing and responding to the actual acts perpetrated against you.

Excluding Blacks from the Biblical history is like removing the cast of characters from a play, and simply allowing the "main character" to recite his lines. To those who fight for the reign of white supremacy, clinging to the "privilege" of superiority, better you stay with that world view, rather than committing some random act of kindness, you know, just in case….. Hedging a bet is a concept that has no place in the Kingdom of God.

TO BE GOD OR NOT TO BE GOD

THE ISSUE OF God versus no God, and all the variations within that issue, is the source of a lot of commentary, opinion, research, both real and imagined, proposed and discerned realities, both "fake" and "real" and other. Is there or ain't there a God? Those with educated, nuanced, philosophical minds can fill out just about all the in between, but for all practical modern , 2020 purposes, there are those who say there ain't, and they are few in number, and those who say there is, and they, are loud in number. After all, if God can't speak up for Himself, they have to speak up for Him, and they know that you have to speak with a loud booming voice if you are going to speak for God. You have to be BOLD in your conversation. God would not have you ashamed of Him, being humble and timid about Him! And likewise, those standing up to those who rant about the perils of disbelief, declaring that it is all "bunk", must be equally loud, if not louder. Those in between these extremes, however, can accept all kinds of half truths, no truths masquerading as truths, or better yet, new "paradigmic" truths, turning Jesus into everything, including a cartoon character, and His father into a cape wearing fighter for truth, justice, and unlimited oil reserves that must be given to the chosen, (who will take it anyway). There are many variations on this theme of "the nature of godliness" that I choose not to offer specifically, because they are all intent on declaring one of two things; rightness, or correctness. You might wonder the difference, but don't ask. It requires many too many words to make a distinction that doesn't exist.

Before we slide down the slippery slope of gibberish, and lose sight of the original premise, let me say that there really is no sense in trying to conclude whether there is, or isn't God. Either with a capital, or a small g, knowing the truth of the matter requires what is required when you watch tv. What is required when you go to an amusement park. What is required when you go to a parade. What is required when you go to a museum, an art gallery, a picnic, a party, a concert, a job, a casino, a shopping center, (indoor mall or outdoor discount center). All require……Your Attention. Actually, when you awaken from the dream that you may have had during your night's sleep, you don't awaken from that dream, but you awaken into the void of the Real world, with a capital W. This void, which is the gigantic IS of that world, which is your reality, speaks to you, in terms that are undeniable, an endless loop of babble, tangential in content and context, ….information which is similar to the following,

> There were some people killed today, some by bombs, missiles, some by starvation, lots, but there were some that died horrific deaths, and the deaths were justified as well as denied by those who caused them, or were

approved by the same. And an old woman became 101 years old today, so don't worry about your children, because other children are worse off, believe me. Anyway, there is one hell of a lot of money floating around, and the people who have it want you to worry about them, but everything is ok. The Dow goes up and down when they get nervous, but they always do well in the end, except when they don't, and then the only thing that happens is that poor people get poorer. Just try your best to look like things are going as well as they can, and understand that the rest of the worlds' problems are just "news to you!", because everything is going well here. And if they're not, they will be soon, so, oh, and if things get bad for you, just relax and maybe do some drugs, but not too much, Just pay attention to the tv, because we are going to be putting on some kick ass programming, hard hitting drama, sexy asexual stuff with hotties, we will be showing ass and cleavage, and gays are welcome!. We have more ways to take your money than you have money to lose, damned you are poor! Can't you get into spending? No problem! We'll show you spending! Big, big,

Bigly spenders, buying $800,000 vacation homes, making money, cheap clothes costing way more than they are worth, and more sex and…… AND,… we will solve all the problems of the world by solving them on fake docudramas, binge series of tv shows that deal with sex, violence, and we will judge the content for you! We will bring on good gays, who love each other, and love for us to be the center of attention. Who is us? Why, you and me, of course!!!! You are you, and I am your brain master, helping you master the madness that tv brings in overwhelming detail, and triviality. Oh, and have I got vacuums..!!!!!

I have vacuums that can suck up a pile of vomit from a weekend drunkfest of 35 college fraternities and sororities, without losing suction!!!! And then milk 21 cows, remove the slime from 32 ghostbusters encounters, pick up two thousand marbles, and still dust the living room floor!!!! Can that same vacuum pick up an F-15 fighter jet and prevent it from taking off????? Let's see……..

I need to go on, and on and on, because that is the way it goes,…. On and on, and on, and on and on. I just can't go on and on with going on and on with that, because that mess drives me crazy. It is mess, and it does drive me crazy. And where were we. Oh yes. We were talking about God. Seems kind of anticlimactic now. That was the fun. That is the gist of the deception. The brain is like a young male teenager in a fast car on a barely traveled, well paved, winding country road. If you asked that male teen to explain the attraction of racing down an abandoned, well paved road in a shiny new sports car, you would not get an explanation. That circumstance needs no explanation. Only a fool would ask what is exciting about the opportunity of racing around a winding road at 125 mph. Well, the only fool that would not ask is the one racing around that road at 125 mph. Wait! What about God? Well. That is the point, isn't it? What about God?

And wouldn't it be wonderful if we could just use this illustration to see how easy it is to lose track of the point, and just lay that conversation about God aside, like putting off putting another coat of paint on the garage. Then we could talk about kids, and fast cars, and how dumb they are, and how they need to grow up, and how they need to accept responsibility for their actions, and how they need to respect the,…. And , and how, and, and, and the next thing you know, we aren't talking about ourselves, ….how wonderful a deception. Not only have we left our own guilt and misery aside, but we have forgotten about all that death and misery that was outlined earlier.

> Oh give me a place, where the buffalo are displaced,
> Where the deer are run over each day.
> Where seldom is heard, any pertinent words,
> And the sky can be full of hay.
>
> Home, home is arranged,
> By the hurricanes, floods, and the flames,
> Where seldom is seen, an encouraging scene,
> And the climate, is never to blame.

"Your comments are bogus. Your attitude is so negative and uninformed. You don't know what you are talking about. You don't understand. You are a weak kneed, snowflake, who doesn't have the sense to realize that the country is great, getting greater every day, under the leadership of the fantastic Donald Trump. If it wasn't for him, there would be big piles of plastic trash all over the ocean, and fish would be dying. There would be radioactivity spilling into the ocean from Fukushima, and climate change would be causing melting glaciers. Obama messed up everything with his Blackness. There is such a thing as blackness. It is what Black people have that can ruin our country, our world. Black people can destroy our lives!!! They can!!! If you don't believe it, ask the monkeys in the zoo. If it wasn't for them, Black people would have been able to get away with making us believe they are real human beings! Yep. I had a 55' Ford Fairlane, dual glass pak exhausts, curb feelers, outside spare with a chrome enclosure, AM FM radio, and then Black people came along and I lost it. They needed food stamps, and they ripped us all off!!! I lost my car. Sad. Sad. So sad."

You are probably thinking that diatribe in quotation marks was very irrational, and silly. You probably think I should not have written any of those last words, nor, and especially nor, included them in a treatise, (if this is a treatise) about the nature of God. You probably think it is showing disrespect having words like sex, ass, in the same paper with words about God. I used to feel that way myself. I even still feel a little nervous doing it. But that nervousness can be overcome when I just stop and think about what is considered information, content, in this world. Donald Trump's tweets are considered worthy of comment. We accept nations as being "Christian", or "Islamic". We speak vows in ceremony, we pledge allegiance to the flag, we are a "nation of laws". Wedding vows ,"till death do us part", and even more sensitive, tearful, emotive vows. We say them. We speak them. We say we mean them. Yet the reality is not only that we ignore them, as time goes by, but that we force those to whom we pledged those vows to ignore them also. Love, honor and obey, decays,,....... Then we complain about our forever spouse's bad habits, the things they don't do. We ignore them, not paying any attention to what they say, what they need, what they might appreciate from us. And as far as obeying, that is out the window. One nation, under God, indivisible, with liberty and justice for all. Just words now. Words without meaning. Words in a tweet. Patriotism?..... Now it is defined as being a Republican. No argument there. No indignation at allowing the meaning of a word like patriotism being dragged through the muck of name calling. A patriot is for building a border wall, and locking up Hilary Clinton. Liberty is for white people. We have indeed come a long way. The extreme is leading the crowd. The tail is wagging the dog. The Christian is being ugly, and the crowd doesn't know the difference.

The crowd? That was gentiles, who were to be led to the truth, and set free. Now they are being led to self destruction. They are being led to hate. They are being led down the path of destruction, because those who lead them have found a market! They are selling righteousness! They are selling "I'm ok and you're not". They have turned their pyramid schemes into tent meetings, with barkers begging, prodding the masses to "get onboard and get rich, and righteous!". The crowd is the fodder for the cannons that fire bombs of self destruction upon their friends, neighbors. It is maniacal madness. Parents, drunk with hype, drag their loved ones down the path, picking their pockets, using their garage to store product that must be moved to generate sales to fuel the massive "downline" of fabricated profiteers. It is "righteousness" branded. At its' best, the movement to monetize desire has no future that isn't self destructive. Why? Because if it makes money, it must at all costs be perpetuated. And when it fails, it strips one literally naked, inviting

A TREATISE OF CONJECTURE ON THE TRUE NATURE OF GOD

catastrophe. Is this about God? Yes. Emphatically. It is about God, because until this all STOPS, there is literally no sense even bringing God, big or small, into the conversation. Pointing to the sky and crossing your heart after scoring a touchdown, only to be tossed aside a few years later, with no help, unable to survive the tomb of concussions, mercifully destroying yourself before that monster left from the "blessed touchdowns" nibbles away what little you have left to live for. God? We hear His words the same way Christopher Walken heard the words of his childhood friend in the movie, THE DEER HUNTER, trying to rescue him from oblivion. If you can just watch that scene, you can see in it the result of a world that has lost touch with "seek ye first the Kingdom". All else will come, but without the kingdom, it doesn't matter what comes. Nothing comes from the light of the Gospel when eyes are already focused on tattoos. Jesus saves when He is recognized. He saves a fool from death in hopes of getting his attention, while the fool brags about having more lives than a cat. Jesus does not rejoice when He hears that they have, "learned their lesson", because when they say it again, they negate that statement. And yes, they will say it again. They will approach rehab with as many different redemptive disclaimers as one can muster before succumbing to the last one. Don't for a minute think that God is enamored with His ability to perform miracles. As Creator, He is well aware of the fact that there are many who have nothing other than intention. "Fitinna". Gonna. This time. And then, more emphatically, "THIS TIME"..... All the time, completely committed, as was Christopher Walken in "The Deer Hunter", to pulling the trigger on that gun wedged against his brain. Is he sure he'll hear a click? Does he think he will escape death? Is that where he is trying to get but failing, thereby enriching himself and the gamblers who bet for or against the gun going off, surrounding him, showering him with cheers or jeers, based on their bet? Or is he in a state of dare...... or worse, simply needing to know when is the gun going to go off and blow his brains out? What does this have to do with the conversation about God? Everything.

Since we are so eager to know this Creator we flirt with accepting as real, let's flip this switch, and find out a little about what it might be like BEING the God that no one believes exists. Having made the only effort possible to let your Creation know that You have some very definite plans for their eternal future, imagine the futility of gathering these "folk" together to move on down the path of eternal enlightenment. Imagine wanting to bless them with a rich and full life, while they reject it and lambast You for bringing them into a situation that they fear may be harmful, and they then seek another god to rescue themselves from YOU! Wow! Let me try to put that in some kind of rational perspective. You are catching hell, and you accept God's help in rescuing you from that hell. But, He isn't coming through with what you believe should be happening, based on your own opinion of what you think ought to be happening, so you lose faith in Him, and let Him know that you are going back to another god, that you didn't even believe in, and if you did, you would only be able to believe that that god really thought you should be a slave, because that is what you were rescued from,.....by this God that actually rescued you from that slavery!!! You MUST,....you MUST understand what I just said. You believed in a God that rescued you from misery. You didn't create this God in your mind! This God came to you, made

Himself known to you, with miracles, signs, etc, almost forcing you to accept that He is real based on the miracles that He performed,……..and here is the kicker, but things didn't go like you wanted them to go, so you made a golden calf sculpture, and went to worshipping that, to get your life back together, where it was. Because,

…..MY HORRIBLE LIFE THAT I WAS GRATEFUL TO YOU, GOD, FOR DELIVERING ME FROM,

. ain't so bad really, because I knew what was going on. I was comfortable there. It is what I was used to. I don't like this thing of depending on You to deliver. I could count on them to provide what little they provided, and I could hustle the rest,…. I can deal with that. This UNCERTAINITY,….. unacceptable. You need a better plan. So. Let's flip the switch back.

Do you wonder why it ought to have taken 39+ additional years to get rid of this kind of insanity that the Israelites expressed when they spied on the promised land and refused to enter it? I think I understand that 40 years is not the issue. God said, " I will not allow one of these people to enter this land I promised them, .IF IT TAKES 500 YEARS TO KILL OFF THE BRAIN DEAD FOLK WHO CAN'T UNDERSTAND WHO I AM, THEN 500 YEARS IT IS………..because my Kingdom is eternal, and eternal doubt and confusion cannot be a part of my kingdom.

THE HYPE OF WISDOM REVEALED..........

SOLOMON. THE KING of Israel. Asked for wisdom in ruling over his people. God credited him with having a great and noble concern, and decided to give him riches, riches he did not request, as well as to give him wisdom. Is he the only man given wisdom? Was he given more wisdom than any other man? As a question being relative to his time, at least Solomon the king points out that he had been given more wealth and wisdom that any of his predecessors in Jerusalem, and did not seem to be making a boastful point of it, but rather, a matter of fact point, which he used as leverage in making his point that "all is chasing after the wind". In other words, he is stating that no matter the amount of money or wisdom, this is the conclusion he has reached as to what he had determined you can get from a life full of wealth and wisdom. Why would God give him more riches than any other before his time? God could have given him wisdom only, since he was already the king of a blessed, chosen nation. This nation was already wealthy, and the king before him, David, was wealthy, so he had great wealth. His statement in chapter 2:12 of Ecclesiastes, reveals his understanding that he was coming "after the king", meaning, I think, he is questioning how much greater can he be, stepping into the shoes of kingship of his father David, who preceded him. But that aside, rather than asking the question, why give him both, which is very tempting to do, let's just simply say,…. so what happened next. Well. He built a magnificent home for both himself and God, parks, manicured grounds, ruled well over his people, indulged himself in every manner of inquiry, seeking to understand many things,… all things,…. Madness, happiness, folly, pleasure, (according to Ecclesiastes), and discovered, in his finite wisdom, that "all is vanity, chasing after the wind..". His advice after living the best of life with all there is to experience for a king, 700 wives, 300 playmates, a queen, a family, luxury and lavish living to the fullest extent of his imagination, etc., etc., etc., ………

Fear God and keep his commandments, for this is the duty of man

I am surprised that THIS man didn't write the song, "I did it my way." He did it his way. That was the statement in Ecclesiastes. That was the message. That is how Solomon BEGAN his reign as king. He sought help from God. He asked for wisdom, and God gave him WISDOM. With that wisdom, God also gave him wealth, abundant wealth. Given enough wealth to do anything your heart desires, it ought be easy to find the desires of your heart. What did his heart desire? 700 wives, 300 concubines, a magnificent palace with all possible luxuries, and, according to Ecclesiastes, to find pleasure, happiness, and meaning in his life. He found himself at the end of his life building idols and worshipping other gods at the behest of his pagan wives. Is it possible for God to provide a man with all possible gifts, riches, of every kind, and have him need a lifetime of living, bathed in that luxury, to conclude that he should believe in the very God that provided the means to it all? It is not only possible, but it is the PRIME statement of fact Solomon the King posed to the rest, including us, who follow God. What is this king passing on to us? There are modern, (which is becoming a dirty word) scholars who attempt to claim that Solomon may not have written this book. Others, also claiming wisdom that disputes, nullifies, casts doubt on the veracity of this book and its' purpose in the Holy Bible, suggest that this message is not on par with the greater "holiness" of the Bible. Yet it is this wisdom that is paramount in understanding the nature of man, and why he, man, must keep more than "family values" in his heart. He must keep the fear of God in his heart, and keep the commandments, to keep in check his, for lack of a better statement, "notions of grandeur." Pride. The very accusation God made against the fallen angel, Lucifer, lurks beneath the surface of the heart of every man and woman, and most every commandment is geared toward keeping that "reality" real. He is born, lives, and dies, and he does so in a cosmos that remains after his death, but he remains, even after death, in a cosmos created by God, and therefore, eternal can be defined essentially by stating that the beginning of the eternal life God states in His word continues the moment after life as we understand it, ends.

With Solomon, we are talking about something that most of us miss. The essence of the daily grind. That search for companionship, home, jobs, careers, things, happiness. The things that make life "worth living'". But when we seek advice from the man who had it all, and could do all that anyone could imagine under the sun, we find him bemoaning all the wondrousness of his life experience as "chasing after the wind", vanity. Could we find a better prophet, a better sage, to speak to this world we live in today? When I look at the statement, "make America great again" and hear, see, absorb the vision spoken by those who wear the hat of the Trump Administration, and those who support and believe in it, …..the words, most every word, spoken by King Solomon provide the very lens needed to view this made again America, in the making. Chasing after the wind doesn't even touch the reality of the Trump Administration. Solomon had the wisdom to seek the nature of living, and report what he found. To Trump, the victor, goes the spoils. And what is yet untouched, will become spoiled, because he has no intent, other than plucking the spoils of victory. His forever campaigning is evidence of his relentless demand to remain in position to reap the spoils of presidential power. With that intent, there is no need for truth, justice, fairness, growth,……. There is only one requirement. Fealty.

And I must keep to the larger message of this treatise, though by no means a greater one in the scheme of this conversation. King Solomon, this wise king, who demonstrated wisdom with his self examination of his life as a king of God's chosen people, was a Black man. Yes. Based on the definition placed on race which has remained stuck in the fabric of the America built on white supremacy, this King would take his rightful place in history as a Black man. Because he is black, we could expect for his words to go unheeded in the halls of modern evangelism. To acknowledge King Solomon as Black and real, and wise, and a messenger to be heeded, would go against the grain of white supremacy that lurks beneath all understanding of history. Furthermore, the Song of Solomon must not be acknowledged, for it seems to suggest that somehow Blackness is involved in the love and sex between two people, one of which, the female, states that she is Black. Her partner, who very much loves and longs for her, is the king himself, and there is no sense in thinking he is white by simply picking one flowery phrase of passion she speaks about him and clinging to it as descriptive of his race. As an interracial couple, or as a Black couple, neither of those notions have a place in the Holy Book for some. Easier to accept the error of placing a curse on the wrong person, Ham and not Canaan, even though the Biblical words themselves describe the truth of that matter, than to accept the words spoken in the Song of Solomon that state "I am Black, but comely…." as being a part of the good Book. I am jus sayin……………

AND THEN THERE'S JOB...............

JOB. ABOUT THIS man I have received the most annoying comments. "The patience of Job…" Where did that come from, and on what line of thinking is patience seen as Job's response to losing his entire family, inflicted from head to toe with painful boils, and becoming instantly destitute because his cattle, herds, etc., were destroyed? Also, I hear from scholars that the Book of Job is undoubtedly the oldest book in the Bible. Not how much older, and nothing about the significance of that fact. At least nothing that I have ever heard. I repeated it myself, just to show that I am up to date with the rest of us with "Biblical Knowledge."

I have read the Book, and in part a few times subsequently, and found a few tidbits of information therein, but I can't say that I really have any more information about that Book than any other cursory observer. So. I am reading it again. Starts with a man that lived in Uz, who was perfect and upright, feared God and eschewed evil. Immediately I notice the phrase "fear God.." That was part of the conclusion of Solomon. Don't know if that is coincidence, or reverberance. What is important to know, I think, is that I don't know. I can't know anything except that notion is stated, and I probably just need to assume that these two people, Job and Solomon, either personify, as is claimed of Job, or testify, in the case of Solomon, in speaking to that issue. I can't find a translation that doesn't state that Job was a very, very good man, and that he was in good standing with God and I assume that evil would be something that he had no part of. God Himself states to Satan a confirmation of the goodness of His servant Job. And as for Solomon, God gave him everything he needed to learn what he learned about God. All the wisdom and the wealth in the world was needed to discover that a lifetime of living could accomplish nothing more than discovering that all that could come from that combination was to realize that there was nothing of value other than to fear God, and do what He says. Once again, the temptation to wrap all this together into one really intellectual, wisdom laden, wealth of religiosity needs to be avoided. Sticking with the text is always appropriate.

Job, was good. Job was a servant of God, and one that God declared was worthy of praise. Job didn't know that God had given him that praise. It didn't take long for him to suspect that praise was the last thing God wanted to offer him. I found it rather odd that Job had the idea that he needed to, and could, sanctify his children after they had the banquets at their homes. He did this because he thought that maybe his sons had possibly sinned and cursed God in their hearts. God stated to Satan that Job was an upright man, and that in fact there was none like him on earth, fearing God and shunning evil. Can it get any better than that? So why does it seem as though this is some kind of proxy war, with Job as the middleman? God says to Satan, my servant Job is the finest man on earth. Satan says, I can break him down and he will curse you to your face. Then it's on! God says "he's yours, take him down if you can." Somehow, this doesn't seem to me to be the message behind this Book. We know how it goes. Satan destroys the man's children, his livelihood, his livestock, and afflicts him with painful boils, which he lances with sharp chards for relief. Then, the finest man on earth, has to reconcile his new position of suffering, misery, sickness, destitution, as the "will of God."

I find in these two men, two sides of the same coin. One, Job, basically asks God, "why did you take everything from me", and the other says, "God gave me everything and it is all meaningless!" Yet, strange as it may be, God says of one, "my servant is upright, there is none like him on earth", and says to the other in a dream, "because you have asked for an obedient heart to judge your people, and not long life or riches or the death of your enemies, I will give you an…".understanding heart so that just as there has never been anyone like you before, there will never be anyone like you again……" . He also made the claim to Solomon that he would bestow riches on Solomon such that there would be no other king like him in his lifetime. Two sides of the same coin. Solomon was the greatest king on earth during his lifetime, also the wisest, and Job was the best servant man on earth during his lifetime. God so stated about them both.

We find these two men, however, deep in despair, one because of his sudden and overwhelming impoverishment, and the other in despair in spite of his unsurpassed wealth!! Two sides of the same coin. It is easy to say "damned if you do and damned if you don't". But damnation is the exact opposite result in both cases. One realizes, in spite of his incredible wealth and wisdom, that fearing God and keeping his commandments is the duty of man. In spite of the possible distraction that wealth and wisdom can cause, "fear God and keep His commandments" is the message of Solomon. The other, Job, after being chided, accused, babbled at by his "friends", who we should say were struggling with the demise of Job, there came the words of Elihu, chapter 38:23 and 24......

Understanding the Almighty is beyond our reach, He is great in power, and He never violates his justice and abundant righteousness.

Therefore people should fear Him, For He does not favor any who think that they are wise.

And then, starting in chapter 38, God, Jehovah, answered Job out of the whirlwind. That was when he was told to "Gird up your loins…." After that incredible conversation, or should I say encounter, with God, Job stood corrected, as did everyone else. Whether truth, fiction, fable, whatever you, in your finite wisdom, would like to make of these two encounters with God, can we agree this…

The fear of God is the beginning of wisdom

Whether we believe it as believers in Him, or deny Him and his reality, we all can agree that this may be the message being sent.

FEAR…….. WHY FEAR?

IF THERE IS one person who needs to grasp the meaning of the concept of God allowing his messengers to make a point of stating to all who will listen, "fear God', it is the person of color who is discriminated against. If ever there is a reason to be thankful that God is not color blind, it is because of us Black folk. That may sound very counter intuitive. We see ourselves suffering with the many years of racism, yet we don't wish to have our eyes opened as to why. We cannot fathom the notion that we may somehow deserve these literal thousands of years of punishment, and we refuse to consider the possibility of that suffering being brought about by circumstances that are beyond our control, yet brought on by our connection to and inheritance of the apostasy of our forefathers, who are undoubtedly part of the Nation of Israel. It is not all Blacks who suffer, but it is all who are Black and descendant of the curse of Deuteronomy. As I said earlier, God does know who we are. He can distinguish between the light skinned child of the Nation from the kinky haired African descended from Ham, as well as being able to identify the coal black Israelite remnant from any and all the rest. There is no racial marker of the Nation of Israel save one,….. most of them were not

Caucasian. Unlike what we see today, a Jewish nation that seems to be simply another subset of Caucasian dominance, the Nation of Israel, historically, and that means from the beginning, not from 1947, was and is a mixture of Hamite and Semite, with very little Caucasian ancestry. Can I prove it? It is not my intention, with this commentary, nor my desire, to convince anyone who needs convincing. If you need to know this, seek this information yourself. I might simply advise that seeking to prove or disprove this fact can awaken a hidden racial bias that can mislead, and misleading is not what this is about. This message, as stated earlier, is for those who may not know who they are, and therefore who ought to seek this information for themselves. So to everyone I say, seek the knowledge that is in the Bible, and seek understanding of how your history may be attuned to the Biblical narrative. If the Bible is referring to you, don't allow anyone to mislead you.

So we look at these two men, and their encounters with God. Solomon, sought the meaning of life, and was given all the tools to find it…. Wealth, wisdom, by the Architect of life, God, Yah, Jehovah. God allowed Satan to take from Job all that there is to life,…home, wealth, friends, health, children, even a future to look forward toward. As a result, I provide to you some of the conclusions Job recited when pondering the changes in his life.

Let the day perish on which I was born

Let God above show no concern for it

Let a rain cloud settle over it

Let no joyful cry be heard in it

Why did I not die at birth

He goes on to state that he could be lying at rest with the dead,.. sleeping with kings who had built palaces that have come to ruin, with princes who possessed gold, and lived in houses filled with silver. He longs for death, even as a miscarriage, and points out that the wicked and the weary are all together, in death, free from suffering, ...prisoners and slaves are free from bondage. They are in darkness, he states, and questions why God would give light to those who are suffering, and life to those who are in distress?? Why do they long for death, he states, and it does not come? Then, in verse 25 he admits something that I find troubling.

"For what I have dreaded has come upon me, and what I feared has befallen me."

When I think back to an earlier statement he made, when it was stated that Job would, (chapter 1), go up to his children after their banquets, send for them and sanctify them, offer burnt offerings for each of them, "for they may have cursed God in their heart", I wonder about his belief in what he was doing. Was he thinking that he was being proactive by preventing God from punishing them by making the burnt offerings on their behalf, even though they may have cursed God?. He states during the long lament in chapter 3 that he dreaded something like this might happen to him. He feared something like this would happen. God was gonna get him. He didn't blame God, he knew that wasn't right. But he wanted to understand why God could be so harsh toward him! Why did this have to happen? There is so much temptation to offer understanding of Job's situation as a bystander, and pontificate about what he thought and why he thought it, but if we just remain with his words, and his actions, can we find something other than the "patience of Job" in his experience? It does state that Job was very rich. All around him knew he was wealthy, and worthy of respect. He was obviously able to perceive in others a real admiration, respect, and maybe even envy. It does not seem, from the text, that Job was arrogant, or thinking of himself as deserving of this favor. He seemed to think that he was blessed by God with all of this, and he needed to make sure that he did everything God wanted him to do, or God might just take all this away from him, and he could be suffering like everyone else. Not only Job, but the entire Book and all the characters in it, except Elihu, were of the same mindset. They were convinced that he had done something that displeased God. Even his wife, I suspect thinking of the misery as something that might continue to worsen, suggested that he "curse God and die", not necessarily with some evil intent, but in hopes of putting a stop to the seemingly endless escalation of suffering. This line of thinking, however, truly suggests a capricious God who can and will punish one whom He protects for reasons unbeknownst to him. As they sought the answer, Job became more and more frustrated, and rightly so, because he was a true servant of God, and knew that there was an answer to his suffering, but that answer was not based on a sin he committed. His final denial of all the reasoning of his friends, but his request for an audience with God, was a true testimony to his faith, his true belief. He did "fear" God in a manner of speaking, for he knew he didn't know why these things were happening to Him, and that he believed he knew God would answer his request for the "why" this happened to him. He had faith in a God who would tell Him, and not a belief that God would destroy him for no reason. In the end, God credited Job for speaking the Truth about him. And that truth? Job acknowledged that he had spoken out of turn, and about things too wonderful for him to understand, and repented. He agreed with God, as he was questioned, that he had no standing trying to question the motives, the ways, the actions of God.

Once again, let's flip the switch, and look at the happenings from the standpoint of God, not assuming that we can stand in God's shoes, but to look at what happened and glean from that a truth about God. We see that God praised Job for being an upright, godly man, like no other, and Satan challenged God, stating that he could break his "servant". God laid out the parameters, and watched Satan try to break Job down with catastrophe after catastrophe. Satan's claim was that he could make Job "curse" him. God gave Satan the opportunity to do so. Job reminded God that he did listen during their encounter, and that he heard God state to him, "who is this who is obscuring my counsel and speaking without knowledge.?" God is outlining that which is impossible for man to comprehend. How can a man understand the workings of God? How can a man know what should and shouldn't be, especially in regard to the making of a member of an eternal Kingdom? There is no reason stated other than the purpose of the law, and the "fear of the Lord" is to guide a man into principles of living that not only please God, but establish in that man behavior that is consummate with the eternity of Kingdom living. From the beginning, God expressed concern with allowing man the knowledge of good and evil to be coupled with eternal life, which he could have obtained be eating from the tree of life. He put him out of the garden and kept guard over it so that very thing could NOT happen. Can this Book bring a lesson to its reader that says, "live with regard for Me, and respect My purpose for your life by doing what I say. Do not think that you are able to understand that which occurs in your life in the context of MY plan. My plan is not your plan.

My purpose is not your purpose. "

At the end of Job's life, he can readily see that he has regained all that was lost, and it is twice as wonderful, and he can also reflect on the fact that he was not forsaken, but went through a trial not only to help him understand that God has purpose that is not seen by man, but that Trust is the fear, the fear to not doubt, nor question all that is occurring, and has occurred, but, as with Job, in all that he did, to not sin, and chose to declare that God may be in error. I ask myself about the angel's conversation with Abraham regarding the fate of Sodom and Gomorrah, where Abraham challenged the destruction of good people with bad people. Giving Abraham the opportunity to plead a case for those few in Sodom who did not deserve to die, God stated that he would not destroy that city if there were 10 righteous people in it. Well, after he moved Lot and his wife and two daughters out, there were none who escaped the destruction. Because God can communicate with man, and listen to man, man cannot assume he can converse with God the way he converses with other men! The answer I would expect to get if I asked Job what is meant by the statement "fear God"? Act toward God as though He is your Master, and you are his slave. Do what He says, and believe in Him, and on Him. He is, and without Him, there is nothing that can be.

NOW, LET"S TAKE A LOOK AT KING SOLOMON………

WITH JOB, SATAN is given the reigns on Job's life to drive him to the point where he will curse God.

Satan's challenge to God is self deceptive. Satan finds himself still in God's graces after rebelling against Him. One would think with rebellion would come immediate destruction. But, as we discovered with Job, we don't know anything about what is going on between God and Satan. We know he is still on the earth, and we know that his time is limited, and he is condemned to Hell, but right now, he is around. I say his challenge is self deceptive because he cannot change the outcome of his existence. Satan's life on earth is finite. From his beginning, he has been present, and will be present until his final days, but he indeed, has a final day on earth with which to reckon. So we must consider that his very presence must have a purpose, otherwise he would be gone. As for Job, his long life ended with the realization that God is, and He is to be worshipped, feared, believed as the only reality.

Solomon, on the other hand, was given another path to follow. He was allowed to seek with wisdom, wealth, and privilege, the nature of life. He was allowed to experience all that there is to experience. He was allowed to indulge in any and every desire of his heart, and do so in a quest for all that can be sought. Happiness, folly, wisdom, the nature of God, and God himself, were options, paths of pursuit that Solomon could choose to pursue. He noticed, observed, tried, built, married, loved, partied, ……did all that he could imagine doing, and nothing, nothing made any ultimate sense to him. Nothing was worthy of pursuit. Nothing had value. He faced the point that Job faced from the exact opposite viewpoint. Two sides of the same coin. Job declared that he knew nothing about God except to fear him. He was humbled by it, awed by it, thanks to a first hand experience. Solomon, however, in seeking all and finding nothing but futility, had to resign himself to the fact that there was nothing "under the sun" that has any substance other that doing the duty man owed God, to believe in him and obey his commandments. Both say that the good and the bad, the rich and the poor, the right and the wrong, all end in the same place, dead.

In the cemetery there are mausoleums housing the bodies of the wealthy, and unmarked graves that bare no evidence of the dead buried there, for lack of money or concern to mark the grave.

If God is, and I say this as a question, I believe He is,.. then His message to us has been carried forward by those whom He has conscripted to do that work. Considering it a figment of the imagination is possible, but if one truly seeks to answer the if to that question, then one must be prepared to deal with what one

NOW, LET'S TAKE A LOOK AT KING SOLOMON.........

finds. Faith, in this process, is always there, because faith is the way we declare all as real, and God is the declarer of His reality. Come away from your search with no evidence of God, you come away with nothing. Beginning your search with the belief He is real, can also be misleading. God does not need your assumption of His reality to be. The command,…. Study, Rightly divine the Word. Seek. Be ready for whatever comes. Be true to what you discover. Believe your findings. Act on them.

What does the Word say? Faith, (the declaring of God as real), without works, (actions based on the belief that God is real), is dead. There is an order, a divine order, to this process. First, you must fear God. And fearing God is clearly demonstrated by two men, Job, and Solomon. They both provide us with the wisdom of the young Elihu. To paraphrase the verses mentioned above,

I am, but you don't know who I am, nor who you are. True wisdom is knowing that. Therefore fear me, because I am the only reality you have. Knowing all else, and not knowing that I am, is truly living in a vortex. When you give up everything in search of Me, you will find yourself, and life. And once you find me, all else will become real.

WEALTH………

LET ME STATE that I find a message about wealth also intertwined not only in the lives of Job And King Solomon, but distinctly tied into the message God delivers to all of us, and it is tied to the statement he made in the Old Testament about His Word, His message to us,…… "….I will put it, (His Word), on their hearts…" With these two men, both paramount, prominent in the Biblical narrative, wealth plays a fundamental role in their ability to listen. Once again. Let's not look at the conclusions we can assume, but at the words written, the words stated to bring about an understanding, an understanding that can be "written on our hearts".

It is the Word that is to be written on our hearts. Love the Lord with all thine heart, soul, and mind. These words are to be in thine heart. This appears in Deuteronomy, (6:5), Jeremiah, (31:33), and Hebrews,

(10:16). The law, the Word, is something that God says needs to be written on our hearts. Love the Lord.

That is the commandment in Deuteronomy. And when we look for clues regarding how to "Love the Lord", we basically hear a statement that, "if you love ME, you will keep my commandments." What should we watch on tv, based on that? What career should we choose, based on our desire to Love God? Where should we live? Should we marry or not.? Who should we marry? The commandments, the law, and the clarification of that Law, the fulfillment of the Law, comes from the son, Jesus. With all that being said, there is not a clear answer to any of the questions proposed regarding what we should or should not do. And there are thousands of other questions, with no clear guidance. But what if the answers are there? What could be the problem with us not being able to glean the answers to those questions? And if some of the answers are there, they are all there. This is God speaking to us. He was speaking to us before there was television. He was speaking to us long before career counseling. His request, I suspect, is primary to our existence. Obeying His commandments is an issue from the beginning of the relationship. Actually, it seems to be all that He wants us to do. In Proverbs, as well as in many other places, the Word is that God knows our hearts. He can search our hearts. He knows why we do what we do, and He knows "the reins" of our hearts. Interesting word. (Revelations (2:23) The reins suggests to me that He knows every act, as well as the intent of every act, and every action taken. Makes me wonder just what is going on. If God already knows everything we do, then what is this business of letting us walk around thinking that we need His guidance? He already knows our thoughts, so it is really futile. If we are thinking that we are doing things the right way, loving, worshipping, and He knows we are not, then why should we even bother trying to "do the right thing"? I am sure you see the deception in this argument. Self deception. You have to believe that it is not possible for God to know us that well to even make that argument. Even worse, you have to think that God can just, "make us right", but that He chooses not to intervene. He can do all things, but He won't make us do the right things. I have to admit to a bit of confusion on my part, in that there was a time when I thought that God already knew who was going to Heaven and Hell even before we were born. He is all knowing. It is futile, therefore, trying to be a believer if you are already destined to be one of the lost? The clue to this seeming riddle is, He knows, not you.

But, following the text, we do agree that we see this notion of God declaring to man that following his Word, His instruction, is THE way to live. Not believing in Him, God, places you in a category best described as MIA. Missing In Action. You are not here. You are present, but not voting. You are in attendance, but you have earphones on, and you are playing a video game, working a crossword puzzle, reading manifestos, binge watching tv on your smartphone, sexting, facebooking, ordering things online from Amazon, drinking, doing drugs. You are mourning the loss of a spouse, a boyfriend, girlfriend, companion, frustrated because your hair is not together, depressed because you are too thin, fat, tall, short, dark, light, white,......, misunderstood, nice, weak, pragmatic, rational, intelligent, ,..... take a moment to add to this list. Think about the amount of time you spend studying, contemplating the Word of God, and the time you spend learning, repeating, believing the words of men you respect, the words of those who are famous, infamous, demanding, politicking, preaching. Think, for a moment, how diligent you are when it comes to seeking understanding of who you are, and whom you are with, and what is going on with them. For a moment, look up from the 51st episode of the tv program. Take off the cool sunglasses, turn off the music, put down the phone, find a spot that has nothing that seeks your attention, or that you cannot ignore for a moment. Turn off the lights, and maybe even, if possible, actually close your eyes, and put noise cancelling headphones on, without plugging them in to anything. Get over the idea of thinking about what could happen if you "disconnect" from the world for a moment. Just stop. Stop it all and be still. For one moment in your life, just be silent, quiet, ……..still. Clear your mind, allowing all thoughts to simply come to rest, so that there is no interference from that stillness

STILL

If I have your attention, so do you. It is at this point, and from this point forward, you are at one with King Solomon and Job. It is from this point you seek to understand the Words of God. Sense, feel, grasp Job, standing before a God he believes in, but quietly, desperately questions his belief. Job has no answer for a question that is fundamental to his very existence, if his belief in God is real, because he wants an answer from God. No one else can provide him any understanding of his experience in life except God. Right before God confronts Job in a whirlwind, Job is at this point. He is still, and waiting for an audience with God. If God doesn't come, then Job knows he has been deceived in his belief. God is bunk. A lie. A fabrication. He will not defend his belief, not fight against it, for he has already accepted it. His belief in God, is real. Remember the coin? The other side of it,

Solomon, is at the same place. Solomon, placed in a pinnacle position in life, king of a people, rich beyond measure, wise beyond the minds of all around him, and being in that position because of an answer to his prayer to God, promising a life of prosperity and wisdom beyond measure. Parenthetically, we must realize that the wisdom God gave Solomon was not in any measure the wisdom God has. However we define it, we have no word that describes the scope of God's wisdom. Solomon is the wisest man, not as wise as God. In all of man's wisdom, and with all of what man, especially modern man, believes is the key to a good life, King Solomon had the best of that. He didn't have a 600 foot yacht like Bill Gates, but he had a fleet of sailing ships. Wealth is relative in that a 7th century B.C. castle will not have electric lights, climate control, all the things we might think are evidence of material wealth. A fireplace to us is for mood, ambiance, not the only way to heat a room. So we must dismiss the relativity of wealth when understanding the significance of what that wealth represented. Solomon's wealth was God given, and abundant to a degree that would have been the envy of all who sought wealth. Solomon had wealth conquered. He had all that wealth could provide. Yet, found himself in a place that, though different than Job, was nevertheless conclusive of the same Truth. In the end, it is God who decides what was done by every man, whether it was good or evil. Job's first family was destroyed. Were they good, or evil? Job was not destroyed. He had as his intention the sanctification of his children after their parties, because he had reason to suspect they may have sinned against God. Those are the words that are printed. Not for us to consider the possibility of his children being sinful. The words state Job's intention. The word also states that, in the end, after Job's encounter with God, all who were his friends and acquaintances, were either chastised, like Eliphaz and his two friends, or came to comfort him over all the evil they had erroneously assumed that God had brought upon him. They also brought him gold rings and cattle, wealth. He was richer in the end than he was before, and Job lived many more years to a ripe old age.

Both men, seeking an answer to the same question, what is the nature of life on earth, discover, when they give their attention to the matter, conclude that God is, and He is to be feared, and obeyed. Fear God the way an experienced seaman, who has sailed the seas many times, knows that it has the power to overwhelm him at any time, and he must pay attention to it at all times. And experienced seaman respects, yes, truly loves the sea, even though it has the ability to swallow him whole, and he sails upon the surface of the sea with respect for it's power, a power that drives him to destinations when properly navigated, and pounds him into its' depths when he becomes foolish and ignores its' warnings. That is the Reality of God, and these lessons from Job and Solomon are indeed evidence of that message.

ATTENTION……..

THAT, IS THE message that resonates throughout the Bible. If I can have you attention please……….. Be still, and know that I am. What can possibly divert our attention from this message? Three things, and we have dealt with one. Wealth is one. Wealth can skew our understanding. I can't deal with all other things that skew our understanding. But as far as attention goes, there are three things that definitely absorb our attention and prevent us from reading, contemplating, seeking, and living with the Word.

Wealth, Sex, and Drugs. We have explored wealth. So let's look at the other two. First…….

SEX..........

THERE IS NO question about the act of intercourse in one respect. Without the climax, the ejaculation of semen from the male into the female, and the concurrent forming of an egg by the female so that the sperm can fertilize the egg, and a definite pathway for the fertilization to take place, there would be no mankind on the face of the earth. That is not to say that God could not have done it another way, or that there are some species that can reproduce in other ways. If there is one thing we ought to know by now, it is that there is no sense questioning the way God has set up the procreation of man. We can, in our modern scientific newspeak, claim to be creating man and animals by invitro fertilization and cloning, yet we know that all we are doing is taking real sperm, taken from real males, and real eggs from real females, and placing them together and them zapping the mix, much like putting two chemicals together in the same pot and watching the reaction. Tinkering with the DNA, adjusting this and that, seeing if we come up with another version of man, or even if we can get to the point where we can take the individual nucleic acids and assemble them into a desired human, whatever comes from all of that research, at this point, is much less than conjecture. We fail our very nature when we seek the far fetched worlds that are wide open spaces waiting for us to conquer, without first coming to a true understanding of the nature of the creatures we already are. What manner of man would we have to be, to be able to deal wisely with the ability to create new beings, when we continue to exhibit a destructiveness that looms over our very existence? Can we bring our white nationalist, every man for himself, everything is ok, live for today even if we destroy the means of those who have to live tomorrow, superior attitude and world view into a new future and expect it to morph into something less self destructive? If we seek to find others who may live in this universe, do we expect to find others like us, who have the same or worse tendencies? Or will we be the ones who are a threat to them? Or do we just think that we are the all in all, and we need not worry about the other planet or planets that have evolved life forms, because even if there are other life forms, we are the "Star Trek", bunch, who " boldly go where no man has gone", and make the Cosmos a better place because of our intervention. Can we see how distracting this fork in the road of understanding can become? First know thyself.

And with that statement, I will delve into the nature of procreation. Of course, there is guidance from the good Book. No need to quote scripture here. There is a general recognition of the sexual experience, and it is an experience many agree should be limited, by the act being placed under the cover of marriage. From Solomon having hundreds of wives, to the New Testament warnings of adultery, there is guidance offered. From the warning of coveting thy neighbor's wife in the Old Testament, to the explanation of committing adultery in your heart when you lust after a woman in the New Testament, adultery and fornication are sins, and that has never changed. Often, marriage is brought about after love has blossomed. What happens in the heart of man, and woman, when they, from the first, see themselves as wanting each other?. Sometimes beauty is the ruling issue. She is a beauty, he is handsome, and that brought them together. The sons of God found the daughters of men beautiful. Abraham's wife was beautiful, Rachael was beautiful, Delilah was beautiful. Bathsheba was beautiful, Rebekah was beautiful. Sampson was handsome, David was handsome, Solomon was handsome. Attractions were and are normal. But do attractions explain everything? Does physical attraction actually explain anything? God obviously did not want there to be any sexual union before marriage. Let's look at the rule. What was there, in the institution of marriage, that allowed sexual unity, yet forbid it without that institution's governance? Without finding the Scripture that documents this, I don't believe there are many of us who don't accept the notion of virginity before marriage as having some merit, and for fidelity to remain the case throughout that couple's lifetime as a positive goal. I should say, that at least most people believe that is the Biblical message. I don't recall any depth of thought given as to why this is or isn't rational. There is a prevailing thought that sex ought not be the initial contact between two individuals, and promiscuity is considered wrong headed. And there is a general acceptance on some level that the number of sex partners ought be limited in scope. Some agree that adultery is a sin, fornication is a sin, marriage is a sacred vow, "you need a family, the Mom and Dad to raise the child". Parenting is about the best non-biblical argument linking sexual purity with a marital relationship.

Well. I think there is much more to this sexual experience than we all admit to, and much more that we accept as right, but ignore. Could we all agree on this? Quietly as it can be kept, the orgasmic experience, short lived as it is, is one of, if not THE most powerful physical, emotionally encompassing experiences we have. I refrained from putting an exclamation point at the end of that sentence, but there definitely is no better sentence to end with that punctuation mark. Let's not talk about what animals do, nor what people do in certain cultures, and let's please, not bring in the experts on this issue. I am just referring to the beginning of that experience, when, in the process of lovemaking, and I am only going to refer to that process, because I do believe that has a Biblical basis, the persons involved sense the inevitability of a climax coming. From that point forward, there is a heightening of intensity, on to and through the climax, and, concluding with those few precious seconds immediately afterward. That is a moment, isn't it. That is the roller coaster ride. There is being excited because you are going to Disneyland. The day before is filled with anticipation. There is euphoria in the air. Anticipation builds on the trip. The airplane ride is fun because the place we are heading to is funner. At the gate, you feel like a racehorse at the line waiting for the gate to pop. Like the dogs at the dog track, waiting for the gate to let you at that rabbit. And then you are off. In line for the Hurricane, the biggest, fastest, scariest roller coaster in the world. You have been on Thunder Pass, Lightning, the Fireball, but the Hurricane,……. Wow! You are on the platform. People are scurrying out of the cars heading for the next high, and you jump in. The bar to keep you safe snaps down on your lap. And then you feel the movement starting, the clicking as the car is pulled slowly up to a height that becomes more and more formidable. Whomever you are with has a look of anticipation on their face. So do you, you just can't see it. You feel it. That car reaches the top, and turns the corner, begins to pick up a little speed. And then, directly in front of you is nothing. That is because, you are finna to go down!!!! What a ride!!! That is the feeling as the car, for the brief and exhilarating moments of whipping up and down, around, and then, coasts slowly to a stop at the end of the ride. And the experience of lovemaking, especially in the early stages, is much like those first roller coaster rides.

Biblically, however, that is just an example of the OE that comes with being human. OE. Original Equipment. That is the way we are set up. That is supposed to be what happens. But here is where we, man, in our distraction with the experience of orgasm, began doing what I will call, aftermarket changes. What we have done to the sexual experience of orgasm, by taking it out of the marital context, has literally altered our ability to understand the nature of God and His plan for us. And I, therefore, assess that as a fundamental error on our part. There was, and is, incredibly, (typical of divine creation), a structure woven into the sexual encounter, and realizing this structure provides an understanding of self, God, and our place in context of living. The seconds after the orgasmic moment, the climax, you are sharing a complete physical, spiritual, emotional connection with the partner. If that moment occurs simultaneously, it compounds the sensation, but each partner experiences that moment both vicariously with the other, or simultaneously, which could be called a mountaintop experience with a volcano added for effect. If we quietly, and fearlessly, think back to any sexual encounter that was particularly enjoyable, all these elements are there. With OE sexual intimacy, we reinforce our love for each other as people, and in the most intimate and powerful way, our love for our mate. Aftermarket, however, sex has become a high. A hit on the drug. It has become so much a preoccupation, that we keep it at the forefront of literally every experience. In our clothing, revealing, in our advertisements, our language, in most things visual, what we hear and say, and discuss, even in our interactions, sex is alluded to in subliminal, but purposeful ways. And the orgasm is like the sweet spot. If we hit it, all the better, but we must work on our swing. If we work at it, we can bring ourselves more satisfaction, but actually, we are simply ignoring the fact that we have turned sex into an addiction, and we have to have it, or evidence of it, around at all times. We live within the matrix of the sexual experience. The sexual experience is no longer within the matrix of marriage. It is literally impossible to find a Church that pays tribute to the magnificence of the sexual experience God has ordained on His people. Discussions about how the two become one? What does that entail? What kinds of things get in the way of the joyous experience of sexual union? Did God intend for us to simply procreate? No one seems to think about the story of Abraham and Sarah, having sex in their old age! No one questions how they knew that Sarah was barren. Did they stop having sex because they tried a few times but since she couldn't conceive, they simply stopped? Within the context of marriage, family, and community, God placed His creation in a perfect plan to become countless, "more than the grains of sand". Countless is what we have become as people. How many have there been on earth? Again. Let's not refer to experts, because there is a number that accurately represents the number of people there have been on the earth, just as there is a number that truly represents the number of grains of sand there are. What is factual, however, is that people have procreated, and there have been a lot of us come and go.

When Jacob wanted Rachel, he was also given Leah. He loved Rachel, but Leah gave him children, and God was all in that, according to the Biblical narrative. God interfered with Jacob's desires, but it is also obvious that the offspring that lead to Jesus are chosen by man's desire for specific women. God allowed Rebecca to help confer Isaac's blessing upon Jacob and not Esau. David committed a sin in getting Bathsheba from her husband, yet Solomon is part of the lineage to Jesus. Throughout the Biblical narrative, there are situations after situations where there is intervention to alter the seemingly normal course of things, and that interference, historically, is responsible for the outcomes we find as pivotal to the Biblical narrative. God has been involved, and still is. As a matter of possible fact, God may be responsible for you being you, for me being me. God may have chosen for your great grandfather to seek the affections of your great grandmother, and continued that until you became who you are. We think of our modern, intelligent selves being able to make "designer babies", and completely ignore the possibility that God has been opening and closing our eyes to each other, steering us, one to another, for generation after generation, in order to create a people to populate His eternal Kingdom. Impossible? Read the Bible, and try to come away with proof of that impossibility. If He is all knowing, and we don't know His ways, let's not speculate one possibility and deny another. So. Based on that, let's get away from speculation about what we think may have been going on, and just look at the record and see what happened.

Marriage has become a ceremony. A celebration. An event. The ceremony takes place in a church on many occasions, yet, the church has very little influence on the direction most marriages take. Infidelity is the only Biblical reason for divorce, yet irreconcilable differences has overtaken this as another reason. But these laws are for believers, not for everyone. Marriage, as laid out in the Bible, is a lifelong connection between two believers, but to many, that no longer is seen as relevant. We have lost the directions. We no longer have the compass of the Word, in the modern world. Sex before marriage is practical, because compatibility is more important than adaptability. Open marriage is a compromise that destroys the institution of marriage. Sex is pornography. Instead of defining sex as relationship, we replace understanding sex through the idea of permissive consent. If two appear to agree with engaging in a sex act, that act is protected as lawful. We allow ourselves to judge whether a sex act, (and sex has been broken down into acts), is "consensual" or not. If not, it is rape, and there are consequences, emotional, spiritual, and physical, the least of which is aborting the pregnancy, though insisting on continuing the pregnancy is potentially very destructive to the victim of rape. We correctly separate sex from rape. But we incorrectly take sexual union out of the format of marriage. There is no longer a commitment to each other first, where the sexual union can then be experienced as celebration of the actual union between two people. Those precious few moments of epilogue directly after the orgasm, confer a stamp of spiritual approval on the relationship where "the two become one". The child, when there is a child, actually becomes a true representative of the genetic union between the two people that merge into one. All that is not stated, but with mutual love between the two, the orgasm can embellish the self concept that a married couple has of self. This self, described as, "and the two shall become one", is a self, that is combination. A self that represents a greater whole. And the institution of marriage forces the attention of the bride and groom upon each other, and upon what they have become to each other.

I stand no better than any other, having gone through the stage of seeking sex for the high it offers, lusting after women. All that has gone wrong with the God intended experience I stand guilty of openly embracing. The smugness of Hugh Hefner, with a "gorgeous babe" on each arm of his silk smoking jacket, was an enviable position. I accepted it, not as my reality, because it wasn't, but as a possibility of encounter. I might find some beautiful girls that would "put out". One that would go "all the way". Like kids playing with fire, even though we had fireproof clothing, (condoms and the pill), the issue of preventing the childbirth ignored the much greater need we all have for intimacy, and the self concept that develops from the declaration of oneness that is marriage. Sex as a skill. Sex as a performance. Sex that controls. The orgasm becomes the disfigured, dismembered, squirting of the male and the moaning writhing of the female. Yes indeed. A penile squirt gun and a vaginal receptacle. The visual of a squirting penis has morphed into a cinematic spectacle, with the male spewing fluid like a crazed gardener, wetting the lips, eyes nose, face, breasts, buttocks, hands, of his lover. Rather than think this scene is disgusting, realize how the internal, biblical meaning I have taken so much time to detail has been trampled. The mind is now confronted with making bliss out of the mess pornography has created. A young female, with an alluring figure, is both target and weapon, depending on the person and his or her purposed desire. A young male also, can be trained by his surroundings to be cunning or demanding, but above all taught that to conquer is to satisfy. The aftermarket is truly focused on the "thrill", and not concerned with the real of sex. The golden rule applies exponentially in the case of sexual intimacy. You definitely do NOT want the man you love having sex with another woman, and if you are the woman, you DEFINITELY DO NOT want another man sharing your mate! If you are LGBTQI, you have not changed the essence of orgasm. How much of this orgasmic experience has changed based on what you determine as real? Find me a person who disagrees, and I will find you a liar. Liars are easy to find. They occupy some of the most prestigious positions in society. They will tell that lie on themselves, but not tolerate being told the truth, if that truth be told.

So we know how intimate the sexual experience is, yet we give up the meaning of that intimacy so that we can enjoy the pleasure of experiencing. That is why it is considered "ok on the down low" for two married people to have an affair. Each cannot commit to the other, because they are already committed to another. It is "safe ground", at least until one desires to ruin it and leave his or her spouse, usually in search of a relationship that has more than "just sex". When you find yourself justifying

SEX..........

a troubling relationship with a phrase such as "the sex is good", you have succeeded in turning a mountaintop experience into a humdrum molehill. Orgasm, like everything else that is part of the work of God, is best understood, and experienced, in context. If you have had the opportunity to have an orgasm with the person you truly love, you will not need to argue this point. And that revelation is the point. What's love got to do with it? Everything.

We have lost our attention span, and fail to know the Biblical message of marriage, fidelity, love, childbirth and nurturing, community, brotherhood…….. the full circle of the human experience, starting with love-marriage-family-love-marriage-family…..and continuing through the lives of all participants.

The two selfs shall become one self. Then, love thy neighbor as thy self. We, therefore, all become one.

DRUGS……..

HOW TO FEEL good? What does it take to feel good? What is feeling good? Happiness? Usefulness? Importance? Wanted? Worry free? What is the best way to describe the basic "World View", station in life,…. Exactly what is "feeling like life is worth living"? How can I describe what I want to discuss? What state of mind, living, is it that one looks for, and, not being able to easily find it, can substitute the euphoria of drugs as a placation? Not really sure what it is. Security? Safety. Contentment? What is the exact nature of that spot that a drug can find, and habitually fill? What really belongs in the spiritual, emotional space, that drug addition so woefully fails to fill? Already have a clue?

I am tempted to start with the scientific, and bring up the role that dopamine stimulation on the nucleus accumbens plays in bringing on pleasurable thoughts. Endorphins, one of the body's natural chemicals that stimulates the brain to have pleasurable feelings, has become common knowledge. But that is not what I am looking for here. The natural drugs the body produces work to provide a good feeling for you. The natural drugs, when one looks at the biochemical manufacturing plant that has been installed in our bodies, provide more than we acknowledge. For example. There are the heroic events that we are exposed to quite often. Military medals are bestowed on men and women who, during the nature of combat, perform what seem to be miracles; i.e., carrying wounded soldiers miles to safety, completely ignoring the misery and disablement they ought to experience from the wounds they receive, have received, and sometimes continue to receive. While there are some who wince, even faint, from the dread of a poke from a TB test, there are others who submit with little discomfort to much more painful experiences as simply a part of what one has to go through. People under hypnosis, a phrase that has become both poo-pooed as well as documented, does offer evidence that is clear; people under a "spell" can nullify pain, follow instructions that can ultimately cause them to lose their lives, or to slaughter their fellow man, and many other acts which, minus the mind altering of hypnotic-like trances, would be either impossible or at least strongly resisted.

Mind control, the phrase, is poorly understood, and I suspect the reason is because once it becomes exactly what it is, mind control, the mind that "controls" the mind control, becomes the evil genius and seeks to "rule the world". Such a simplistic statement ought not stand in a paper claiming to be at least "rational".

Well. I don't claim this to be a rational paper. I don't claim it to be anything. Even the claim made in the title, is nuanced by the word, conjecture, which is defined as "an opinion or conclusion formed on the basis of incomplete information", acknowledges the obvious. I don't know anywhere near all there is to know about the nature of GOD. But what I do know, and can claim, is that the dialogue, such as it is, we share in 2020 about almost anything, is peppered with self serving "factoids", distorted wives' tales, (whatever a wives' tale is), propagandistic jargon, soundbites with little or no basis in fact, screamed as diatribes and slogans, repeated slogans hastily made during heights of tension, ... yes, and that can include this, has displaced understanding. The only defense I have against considering this treatise as simply another part of the collective "rant" of the whirlwind we call dialogue, is that it is considered. I have taken the time to offer this as what I state it to be. Take the time to read and consider, as a reader, your response.

Mind control. Nothing new. Let's take the words we hear and say, in much the same way this work has taken the Words of God. Look at the data. What happened. What is the result? In many cases, one can see the purpose more clearly if one looks at what happened as a result of words spoken. What does this have to do with the nature of God? Let's ask a few questions and see if there can be any clarification.

Words. "I pledge allegiance to the flag, and to the republic for which it stands. One nation, under God, with liberty and justice for all." The history of this pledge, meant to be used by any nation, written in 1892 by a socialist, Frances Bellamy, was appropriated in 1923 by adding the words, " the United States of America", and, in response to the communist threat perceived by President Eisenhower, was altered in 1954 by adding the words, "under God", reveals the underpinning of the words which we have had placed on the lips of our citizenry, and slowly but surely, ignored. How can we hear, and say, these words, yet ignore them? Which words? How about liberty and justice for all? Please don't start with that babbling madness about who has done what, or how it was never the intent....., please. Stop. This is not on facebook. There is no line at the bottom for reactions. This is not the place for talking points. YOUR hypnosis, not mine, is responsible for the knee jerk response built in to you by those who have found a friend in "mind control". A friend? Yes, a friend who rewards handsomely for aiding and abetting the control of YOUR mind. If that is where you are, please lay this document aside, and find another place for your hypnotic spell to flourish.

These words are part of the fiber of America. A nation that believed in a god? A special God? Is that America? Well, let's look at what happened.

By 1892, slavery had been officially abolished, although most, ostensibly all, of the underlying beliefs about the Black man as inferior, indeed accepting if not deserving of a 2nd to 3rd class existence, as well as the authorized mistreatment of the black man and woman, remained well into the 20th century, and many remnants are still present. Also. "Your tired and your poor", words written on the Statue of Liberty, have been altered by a statement of the current administration to exclude those very people. You cannot be poor and tired, but self sufficient. Fleeing tyranny, while having the capacity to obtain health care, money to support yourself, does not really match the intent of the statement, and those who wish to justify it ignore the duality of their argument. Hispanics, Muslims, Africans, Haitians, ... The list is getting bigger as the world becomes more and more unwilling to face the shortcoming of reducing the rank and file citizen to serfdom. That is not happening? On any given day, I can turn on any news station, look at any reporting by people at the scene, (or ignore it like some "news" organizations), and see that literally people in the millions worldwide are in the streets protesting one thing or another.

So WHAT IS THE POINT???? What is this rambling about. People are not happy. People are not in the streets, facing police with guns, tear gas, clubs, arrest, because they are happy and content. People are not in the streets because they are given the day off to demonstrate. People are not in the streets because they are afraid that the "good life" is going to be taken away! However you spin it, they are searching for a life in their country that is more in tune with "liberty and justice for all", however you spin it.

If we are willing to accept the actions we see world wide as expressive of a truth, that truth is about what they have lost and seek to regain. There were no middle class revolts when there was a middle class that could buy a house, provide for a family, pay for the food, clothing, shelter they needed and were satisfied with having the freedom to "pursue" the best of life. They bought cars, paid off loans taken out for homes, cars, furniture, they purchased. They were happy with that. There was even room for the immigrant, the African American, though to a lesser degree, to experience what the middle class was, a word that has a silent adjective, white, as a preface. Understanding that Blacks and immigrants never had this freedom to the degree that Whites had, one ought to assume that it was not Blacks and immigrants who took away this right. No matter how much one may believe that the cost of Welfare has taken away their middle class status, looking at those who are supposed to have "stolen" the wealth of the middle class by government giveaways, it ought to be easy to see that this money does not appear in their lives. They are not driving Cadillacs, spending money at the rate the white middle class had been comfortable spending. Furthermore, to state that there are one thousand people who have figured how to "game" the system, ignores the fact that the slice of the Government devoted to public assistance is much, much too small to blame for the demise of the middle class. Corporations stealing the retirement funds through mergers, biting off the union's hand in achieving reasonable work weeks and compensations to spite the face of the very workers who fought for these concessions would be a more reasonable explanation. And hearing the claims of welfare fraud from the very politicians, who silently raided every penny from the largest fund ever generated in the history of mankind by the individual citizens acting cooperatively in giving a portion of their income for future benefit, the Social Security system, and replacing it with an IOU, with not one signature from a participant in that theft, is another reason to stop blaming Hillary Clinton or Donald Trump for this crime. It goes without saying that blaming Black people for the welfare system that is used far more by whites than any other group of citizens is not wrong headed, it is no headed, period.

So what does all this have to do with drugs? And what does that have to do with God? There is a promise in the bible. A promise

God offers to any and all who accept Him by believing in His Son, and a promise that has been kept to those who lived by His commandments in the Old Testament. He stated to them that He was not giving them the land He promised because of their righteousness, because they were an obstinate people. He was taking the land away from the current inhabitants because of their wickedness. He provided the tablets with commandments on them. He did that twice, because Moses cast the first set carved in stone on the ground when he saw the rebellion of the Nation against God. What is the promise? He will be your God. Live life according to His commandments, fear Him, trust in Him, and your life will be good. What does that mean? Well, let's look at the results. First, with those who believe and do his commandments, and then to those who do not.

Anyone we know who we can say is a believer and doer of the Word? They are around. They live in the same world as those who don't believe. They have children. They have careers, jobs, homes. They have what those who don't believe have, and more. Not the material things. You can measure those things with one against the other. The person who believes has the one thing that makes all the difference in the world. They have God, and all that comes with it. Promise of eternal life, with resurrection at the end times. All other needs being met because of your belief. All things working together for good. A very high bar. And that is the false promise of drugs. Take them, and for a moment, you'll be in heaven. All worries will be gone. You will have what you need, but only because you can't really find a need for anything except another hit to get you back to where you were, when you were in "heaven". The high, lifts you out of all pain and misery. It doesn't fill your stomach, but distracts you elegantly from your hunger. It doesn't give you rest, but it does make you think that you simply don't need it. You have better things to do than sleep. The abundance of material wealth in the world allows you to simply take what you need, without paying for it. Even the drugs ought to be free. They are not, but you can die trying to make them free. Your life is only a mess when you run out of drugs. Another hit, and you are propelled back into nirvana, and things are right again, until they are not. Then your need more to feel a little closer to that place where you used to achieve easily when you first used drugs. And slowly, but surely, you need more and more, to feel less and less high, until you finally find everlasting nirvana, or a wake up call in the hospital. And then, you only have two choices. Certain death from overdoes, or certain misery from withdrawal. Meanwhile, what we would call a life,.... Things like home, spouse, children, friends, relatives, all is gone or in shambles by being hooked to the same wagon as you. Though there are those few who claim that they have survived on drugs, never lost their job, went to work every day, they often fail to mention the things we all would like to have. A great relationship with a spouse, wonderful kids, nice house, an interesting, fun filled, meaningful life that has been and still is rewarding. A smile on the face and a pep in the step, good health and long life, ... Kind of makes the, "I kept my job" proof of life a little lacking. So, to reiterate, from having all the material wealth of a king, (Solomon), to having all you have taken away, (Job), there is nowhere to turn in spite of nor because of, other than God. I can say, from having watched drug victims come and go in county jails for well over 31 years, that my experience has been that those who find God, not just a higher power, but the God of the Old and New Testament, along with and usually through His son, Jesus, have a much higher percentage of overcoming drug addiction than those who say they "have a responsibility to their kids, wife, family, know better, slipped, have been clean for days, weeks, months, years…" You do not know what you have missed until you find God. You don't know what you have until you fear Him, and trust Him enough to obey His will. You will certainly succeed in finding Him if you die seeking Him. And when you find Him, you will never die.

GETTING OUT OF THE WEEDS.......

WENT FISHING WITH my dad a lot when I was growing up. Sometimes I notice that people both reflect upon as well as seek to glean a lot from their childhood experiences. Sometimes I notice that they don't even realize the depth of experience they had during childhood. Sometimes they don't realize how damaged they had become from childhood, and vice versa, how much their childhood experiences had been a blessing to them. That is because we all come FROM the experience, and we all are in the trees, and are not able to see the forest. It isn't until we literally begin to "compare" that we realize what we had, didn't have, want, no longer want, avoid, and sometimes, unknowingly seek.

Fishing on an inland lake, we always searched for the weeds. My job was to lean over the front of the boat and let him know when we had begun moving into the weeds. His idea, and I learned it from him, was to fish just off the weeds. Do not fish in the weeds. You can catch a lot of fish, but they are not in the weeds, they are moving into and out of the weeds. How he knew that I don't know. Was he right? Let's look at the result. We ate fish every Saturday, probably from May till October, and they were always fresh on Saturday. Caught in the morning, cleaned and fried at noon, eaten at 3:00 pm. Never had a day I recall when we had no fish to eat. A few days, there where hot dogs that filled us more than fish. His knowledge basically worked for our needs. We always parked just off the weeds. We also watched the others who were fishing. Sometimes we would discover that there were other fisherman who were catching fish when we weren't. My dad would ask them what kind of bait they were using. Some would be helpful. Other times, no matter what bait you used, there would be some days when you didn't catch many fish, and other days when you would catch a lot. There were times when they would bite, and times that they wouldn't, and we didn't always know when that was. There was one spot on that lake, however, he found, by watching people fish. He noticed that they would go to that place every time they came to the lake. He used landmarks and perspective to locate that spot, and after a few times, we found that there was a hole just off the shore. We were cruising toward the shore one morning, and I began to see the weeds, so I reported that to Dad. Then, when we got ready to drop anchor, the weeds disappeared! I told him they were gone, and he listened to his 8 year old child, and drifted slowly closer to the shore, to see if we found weeds again, which would have been unusual, I now realize. When we found them, we dropped anchor and fished toward the spot we had just left, where there were no weeds. It was a hole, rather deep, right off the shore, right in the middle of the weeds. I never took credit for helping find the hole, because I was too young to realize what we had found, and the implication of that finding. But we caught a lot of fish from there. I wasn't too young to notice that we were catching a lot more fish! Now I realize that there were local people who knew of the spot, and would go there and fish. We didn't know it existed, until we found it. We weren't alone. All the evidence was there, for anyone who had the will to look, and the attention span to notice that some fisherman were sitting in the boats catching nothing, while others were catching fish. Someone had found it, and they knew not to put a billboard over the spot and invite everyone to come and fish it dry. Just fish, eat, and enjoy. Do not destroy.

I can tell you something I learned about fishing in the weeds. You catch a lot of weeds, and the fish you catch are usually smaller, and can get away by tangling you up in the weeds. For us, fishing in the weeds was counterproductive. We needed to STAY OUT OF THE WEEDS.

What does this have to do with our relationship with God? Well. I think it is a message to those who are fishing. Seek, and ye shall find. That is a message from Jesus, the Son of the God, we are invited to seek. There is a parable about seeds sown in the weeds. They thrive in the beginning, but their lives are cut short, and off, literally choked off by the rapidly growing weeds all around the seedlings. The message of this parable, however, is a message to someone I don't know. It might even be a message to me. The reason I don't know who this message is intended to reach, is because I, as well as they, don't know who they are. They know their names, their friends, their family members. They know where they live, the street address. They know their telephone number. They know a lot, but they don't know from whence they came. They don't know their history. They don't know history. They don't know the lake, because they don't know that fishing the lake, for food to eat, is not a promise you will eat. They have not paid attention to the world around them. If we were to seek these people out, we would most likely find them struggling to survive, and they would be, figuratively, fishing in the weeds. They will most likely catch small fish, along with lots of weeds. And if weeds can be considered vegetable, they would be vegetarians who eat a little meat. By every measure in life, they will be found lacking. If God be real, and I believe He is, (even without being asked, He stated, "I AM"), these people would be, figuratively, fishing in the weeds. They might say things like, "I just want what all the rest of these fisherman around me have,". They see others and assume that having a boat with a motor will be what they need. A fancy spinning reel instead of catching fish with a cane pole. Let's spend a little time with them, and hear some of their conversation..........

"I am being denied my rights. The rights that you say I have, I am being discriminated against! You are treating me wrong! You have done many cruel things to me. You raped my wife, held us as slaves, brutally hung us. You did horribly cruel things to us. Because of the color of my skin, you treat me like an animal, and you do it without considering me human! All I want is a little of what you have. The right to seek life, liberty, and happiness. A piece of the pie. You write laws against people who do what you do to us, but you exclude yourselves from the law. When we kill you, it is murder. When you kill us, you only violate our civil rights. You steal our wealth from us, then arrest us for taking a loaf of bread."

This rant can go on and on. It is horrible. It is well founded. It is a true statement. And, it is Biblical. It is not, however, simply nor only because of the color of their skin. The people who enslaved Blacks used the color of their skin to identify them. But they were enslaveable. What a weird thing to say about people. They were easy to enslave. But how could that be? What can make a person enslaveable? Well. There are some things that can happen to people that make them easily identifiable as having no identity. No home country. No place to belong. If you have no place to belong, then everywhere you go is a strange land, and someone else's land. No government to fight against enslavement. No protection offered for people in this predicament. For some reason, they have no power to stop anyone from conquering and enslaving them. They are like orphans who run away from the orphanage. Where do you go, if you are an orphan, when you run away from the place that is taking care of you? You have no family that you know. You have no country that you know as yours. You have to go where others will allow you to go, or say you belong, and if they don't know where you belong, then you are just out there, homeless. Without a home, … a place to belong to, and come from. Without a history to reflect on, and remember, you simply do not belong. But you have a past. Everyone has a past. Actually. What is the difference between an orphan and a beloved child? Both have parents! Oversight. Both children need oversight. Everyone can agree that a child, a newborn, must have some kind of oversight. If true, even the child born in the wild, in order to survive, the role of oversight is managed by those in the wild,.... Wolves, bears, tigers. There are stories, I am sure many are to some extent exaggerated, yet the concept cannot be more real. An abandoned baby, without some kind of oversight and nurturing, cannot survive. What does this have to do with God, and how many times does this question have to be asked? Well, this has to do more with getting out of the weeds. To the point. The Nation of Israel was a nation, chosen by God, best explained by Deuteronomy in chapter 7. This Chapter describes who the Nation is, where they were from, and why God has chosen them. It is better described in detail elsewhere in the Bible, but I find this chapter explicit in stating that the Nation of Israel consists of those people who were enslaved in Egypt, who were the direct descendants of Jacob, (Israel), and they are, therefore, those 70 who entered Egypt to live, and multiplied and "filled the land". The major part of the Book of Deuteronomy deals with two very specific promises by God to these people. One is a promise of what will happen to them if they heed the laws, fear Him, (covered earlier), and the other, is a negative promise. The negative promise is, if they chose not to heed Him, if they do not fear Him, decide to worship other gods, turn away from Him, He will bring curses upon them. And starting with Deuteronomy 28:15, these curses are laid out. Reading them, one cannot disagree that being "orphaned" could well describe this experience, especially since God states from that point forward, that He wishes to have His chosen come back to Him! A child orphaned at birth cannot be blamed, nor held responsible for the mother and or the father abandoning it. Nevertheless, a child orphaned, and through generations, not ever knowing his or her actual birth parents, could come to believe that he or she is of a community, or generation, with which he or she has no genetic connection. This is not only possible, but has often happened, and simply explains what, why, and how the world goes round. Many are parented by someone other than their birth parents.

The Nation of Israel, that grew from 70 to multitudes within Egypt, consists of 68 males, and two females, mating with the women and men of Egypt, over 400 years, to produce a multitude of shemitic/ hametic people. To argue whether these people, the Nation of Israel, were somehow "Caucasian", is the quintessential fraud nurtured by the delusion of "whiteness" being conflated with everything grandiose. Once again. God knows each and every one of these people, and can trace each and every one of them through generation after generation, up to 2020 AD. And His message CLEARLY lays out His ability, through His son, to bring a message of reclamation in the form of the Gospel, to all those who are to be a member of His Nation, the Nation of believers in Him. Every word just stated in this paragraph being true, this fact is not a warning to anyone who is Black that might wish to "get on board", nor an exclusion to any who find His Kingdom by belief in His son. The greater message, stripped of the "weeds" of religious dogma, real and "fake", is that God knows the heart of man. God is. He is what He says He is. We do not know Him, like we know each other. We do not even know each other well. If there is anything we can glean from the seed of the Nation of Israel, living in the weeds of modern society, it is the fact that race can be the true tool to help identify the lost of the Hebrew Israelite Nation. That Nation was Black, and the remnants of it are best identified as Black, by any racial measure. We can speak of heaven, and eternal life. We can believe or cast doubt on the miracles performed, the parting of the sea, the resurrection from the dead. We can study the words of learned men, seek knowledge, research the very nature of our selves, from our loftiest goals and aspirations to the nano particle biochemical essence of our physical presence. We can do all we do. We can see all we can see, and daily find more that we didn't realize existed, and accept it as real. We can also go beyond our understandings, whether as fantasy, or in newly experienced realities. Our "limitlessness" is actually what limits our understanding of God. We are free to think and do what we will. There is no mindset beyond our own. That, is the massiveness of the "weeds". That is how wide "is the road". And God, in seeking the Lost, is expecting to find people of color. All colors. All colors of man can come from these people, and the Nation most likely is represented by all colors we know of as man, yet through the eyes of race, we must admit that truth will force us to see Black and Brown people as an integral part of that Nation, as well as of humanity.

Once again, and these are not my words, but the words that can bring any of us to an understanding of who we are and what we are to do here. Our true calling. To all who claim to believe in the God of the Old And New Testament, understand that the phrase ""the times of the Gentiles" speaks a Truth to this modern 2020 society. There is no explanation for there to be a worldwide outrage for the mistreatment of George Floyd that fits better within this context than the end of this "time of the gentiles". If this is truly a "Nation under God", the growing intolerance for the racist mistreatment of African Americans, coupled with the loss of the oppressive grip held on Black and Brown people by White supremacists world wide; the hold these white nationalists maintain on the white evangelical community in America; the falling away of European domination from the True Church, of which Christ stated the "gates of Hell would not prevail against it", …..ought be an awakening, an invitation to all, White and Black, to revisit the scripture with purposeful intent. The purpose?

Be still, and know, that I am God. Fear me, and obey my commandments.

Love the Lord, thy God, with all thine heart, mind, and soul. This is the greatest commandment, and the second is like unto the first. Love thy neighbor as thyself.

The commandments apply not only to unborn babies, but to the poor, the imprisoned, the sick, the immigrants risking their lives fleeing death and destruction in their native countries, the eradication of means of survival from the working poor to fatten the coffers of the rich. If I continue to list all the evidence that abounds in this world of neighbor mistreating neighbor, I only chronicle the present state of affairs. If the Word of God can prophetically warn against a society developing into what ours has become, long before it came into existence, what does is say, in prophesy, about the result of not heeding that warning?

Yes. Revisit the Word. Not with the aid of an interpreter, but with the Guide provided. The way is there to find. How would one know? Simple. John 14:6. I am the way.

> If you have come to embrace white supremacy in your search for God, ...
>
> If you have found white supremacy an obstacle to believing in God..................

Take some time to stop, close your mind, open your heart, by silencing all that comes into mind. and be still. Be still, and know, that....

> "Out of the abundance of the heart, the mouth speaks"

Lightning Source UK Ltd.
Milton Keynes UK
UKHW012005181122
412457UK00013B/186/J